Nurturing Paws

Edited By Lynn C. Johnston

A Whispering Angel Book

Nurturing Paws

Copyright © 2011 by Whispering Angel Books as an anthology.

Rights to the individual stories and poems reside with the authors themselves. This collection contains works submitted to the Publisher by individual authors who confirm that the work is their original creation. Based on the authors' confirmations and the Publisher's knowledge, these pieces were written as credited. Whispering Angel Books does not guarantee or assume any responsibility for verifying the authorship of any work.

Views expressed in each work are solely that of the contributor. The publisher does not endorse any political viewpoint or religious belief over another.

All rights reserved under International and Pan-American copyright conventions. No part of this book may be used or reproduced by any means, graphic, electronic, or mechanical including photocopying, recording, taping or by any storage retrieval system without written permission of the publisher except in the case of brief quotations embodied in critical reviews and articles.

ISBN-13: 978-0-9841421-6-3

Whispering Angel Books
7557 West Sand Lake Road #126
Orlando, FL 32819

http://www.whisperingangelbooks.com

Printed in the United States of America

Whispering Angel Books is dedicated to publishing uplifting and inspirational works for its readers while donating a portion of its book sales to charitable organizations promoting physical, emotional and spiritual healing. If you'd like to learn more about our books or our fundraising programs for your charity, please visit our website: www.whisperingangelbooks.com

"Until one has loved an animal,
a part of one's soul remains unawakened."

~ *Anastole France*

TABLE OF CONTENTS

DEDICATION iii

ACKNOWLEDGMENTS v

INTRODUCTION

Lynn C. Johnston vii

PERFECTLY NORMAL

Sara Barker 1

BUDDY

Chuck Willman 5

TRANSITION

Sandra Ervin Adams 6

SENSE OF COMFORT

Carolyn T. Johnson 7

DO NOT DELETE

Deborah Schildkraut 8

A GENTLE HEALER

Nikki Rosen 11

BAILEY: A GOLDEN RETRIEVER

Paul Cummins 13

THE GIFT OF TEARS

Alan Pratt 14

YOU MEAN THE WORLD TO ME

    Ruth Sabath Rosenthal 16

MIRACLE

    Lynn C. Johnston 17

THE SEEING-EYE MAN

    Paul Sohar 19

MY DOG IS SPIRITUAL AND ETERNAL

    Justin Blackburn 20

MISTIE'S MAGIC

    Beckie A. Miller 21

THE TIME OF HEALING

    Willard Stringham 23

CATAPLEXY

    Cristina Ferrari-Logan 25

HEAVEN SENT

    Suzanne Manning 26

A GREGORIAN KIND OF A CAT

    Elaine Morgan 29

ISIS

    Mark McGuire-Schwartz 32

A PLACE IN THE HEART

    Scott Peterson 33

BLACK DOG

Wendy Wolf..35

CALYPSO

Holly Day..36

LADY'S LOYALTY

Glenda Barrett..37

FIERCE ATTACHMENT

Tina Traster..39

FELINE THERAPY

Sandra Ervin Adams...42

STATE FAIR

Paula Timpson...43

FLETCHER

Barbara Moe..44

PUPPY LOVE

Madana Dookieram..47

ALL DOGS DO GO TO HEAVEN

Tammy P. Stafford..48

AN ORDINARY BOY

Rebecca Taksel...51

AUTUMN WALK IN MIZZLING RAIN

Nina Romano...53

CARPE DIEM

    Michele Krause 54

IN WITH THE NEW

    Kathleen Gerard 57

NEW DOG

    Nancy Brewka-Clark 60

FLOWER POWER

    Cona Gregory-Adams 61

GOLDEN BOY

    Lea Gambina Pecora 63

MAX

    Rosemary McKinley 65

HOW A BROWN BABY BUNNY CHANGED EVERYTHING

    Sarah Goodwin-Nguyen 67

WHO?

    Rosalie Ferrer Kramer 69

IN MY DOG'S EYES

    Paul S. Piper 70

PEPPER: THE PROSAIC PIGEON

    John R. Chega 71

DEVOTED EYES

    Louise Webster 75

THE LANGUAGE OF LOVE
> *Judy Kirk* 76

THE GRAY GHOST
> *Elaine Morgan* 77

DREAM GIRL
> *Elynne Chaplik-Aleskow* 80

ANGEL BOY
> *Jean Varda* 82

CARING FOR TEDDY
> *Diana M. Amadeo* 83

REST, MY SWEET GIRL
> *Linda O'Connell* 86

SPUNKY
> *Cherise Wyneken* 87

MITZI AND HER MEN
> *Erika Hoffman* 89

OUR CANINE FAMILY MEMBER
> *Francine L. Baldwin-Billingslea* 93

THE TOUCH
> *Carol J. Rhodes* 95

MY MUSE
> *Carolyn T. Johnson* 96

A WINDOW TO WISDOM
>   *Lynn Pinkerton* 97

REMEMBERING SASHA
>   *Nikki Rosen* 99

RUDY ON A SATURDAY MORNING
>   *Gayla Chaney* 101

SUNSHINE SAMMY
>   *Annmarie B. Tait* 104

LITTLE OWL OF WATCHFULNESS
>   *Penelope Moffet* 107

THE EAGLE HAS LANDED
>   *Edward Louis* 109

OH FUDGE! ANOTHER NUDGE!
>   *Terri Elders* 111

FALCON'S EYE
>   *Madana Dookieram* 114

PURRING, HOW, WHY, AND WHY NOT
>   *Maren O. Mitchell* 116

WHAT YOU MEAN TO ME
>   *MiMi Q. Atkins* 117

STREAK: THE PARROT WHO LOVES ME
>   *David O'Neal* 118

SILVER SAINT

    Deadra Krieger 121

UNLIKELY DUET

    Cona Gregory-Adams 123

PURRS, PAWS AND CAT SCRATCH KISSES

    Sheree K. Nielsen 124

THE CALF

    Christopher Woods 127

THE SENTRY

    Judy Kirk 128

THE COLOR OF LOVE

    Martha Lavoué 129

UNDERCOVER CAT LOVER

    Dwan Reed 130

RUNAWAY

    Mary Borsellino 133

NURTURING PAWS

    Paula Timpson 135

THE LINK IN MY LIFE

    J.C. Howard 136

THE CHOSEN ONE

    Nadia Ali 139

SPECIAL VISION – NOT SPECIAL EFFECTS
Rebecca Groff 142

SERENITY
Linda Blasko 145

LITTLE TINKER
Jean Varda 146

THE BEGINNING
Kellye Blankenship 147

NEVER TOO LATE
Ronda Armstrong 148

RALPH
Ben Humphrey 152

HOW MY CAT HELPED SAVE MY LIFE
Aphrodite Matsakis 155

MY OLD LOVABLE NEW FRIEND
Susan Berg 157

ABOUT THE CONTRIBUTORS 159

WE WANT TO HEAR FROM YOU 175

DEDICATION

This book is dedicated to the animals that have graced my life: Josie Jo, Cross, Valentine, Tessa Rose, Boo, Fred, Morris, Dusty, and Joshua. Each one has taught me the meaning of love, compassion, loyalty, gratitude, forgiveness, and friendship. Without them, and all the animals honored in this book, *Nurturing Paws* would not have been possible.

ACKNOWLEDGMENTS

The creation and development of this book would not have been possible without the assistance of many people. I would like to thank everyone who submitted their heartfelt stories and poems for this anthology. With hundreds of wonderful pieces to choose from, each prospective contributor made the selection process far more challenging and rewarding than imaginable.

My deepest appreciation goes out to Julie G. Beers, Bob Bergstrom, and 93-year-old Salina Bergstrom. Their opinions, support, and expertise were invaluable during this process.

INTRODUCTION

Roger Caras, the host of the Westminster Kennel Club Dog Show, once said, "Dogs are not our whole life, but they make our lives whole." I think that can be said of all animals. As most animal lovers know, pets play a crucial role in our lives. They are not just four-legged or two-winged occupants in our home; they are members of the family.

Unlike their human counterparts, we can always count on these family members to be completely genuine and unaffected by the outside world. Our cat will never care about our occupation; our dog won't judge our social status; and our bird won't give a hoot about our lifestyle choices. And we'll never be able to impress any of them with our net worth. No wonder we love our pets! How many people can you say that about?

Scientific studies have long since confirmed the beneficial effects of pets in our lives. Having a pet has been proven to reduce stress, lower blood pressure, ease anxiety, and uplift our moods. Pets also help us feel less lonely and often increase our own physical activity as we simply care for their needs. It's even a proven fact that pet owners live longer and healthier lives.

You only need to spend some time with an animal to learn that they are the very definition of unconditional love, loyalty, frienship, forgiveness, gratitude, and acceptance. They take life one day at a time and face life's challenges with tenacity and an unbridled spirit. And if that isn't enough, they are compassionate creatures with a keen perception of our needs. Most people could all learn a lot from their example.

The short stories and poems in Nurturing Paws are powerful testimonies to their remarkable abilities to ease our physical and emotional pain.

I hope that in reading these wonderful pieces you'll take away a greater appreciation for the power in their Nurturing Paws.

~ Lynn C. Johnston

PERFECTLY NORMAL
By Sara Barker

    I was just his co-worker when Fontana broke her spine. Other than in pictures, I had never seen her spunky, impish face, all black with tan Doberman spots, and her snout panting in a wide pink grin. When I met her, she looked nothing like the knee-high companion from the photos around his desk. She was immobile, half-shaved, with staples piecing together a raw seam bisecting her the long way.

    The trouble was keeping her clean when she had no bladder or bowel control and could not change her position. The trouble was keeping her playful, gregarious spirit exercised when her body couldn't be. The trouble was that Fontana's broken back was the straw that broke the back of his already floundering marriage and that when his wife left, the burden of being the sole caretaker for a paraplegic dog recovering from surgery fell completely onto him.

    My sons and I helped out every day after school. Fontana would greet us enthusiastically, as if her pillow were a royal throne she sat on by choice and her subjects had just arrived to provide amusement. Her eyes sparkled and shone as the three of us climbed into her metal pen. While I cleaned weeping bedsores, she pawed happily and snapped at the toys the boys held just beyond her reach. I watched her strength return to match her spirit. I watched how she stretched towards the squeaky squirrel they held, how she leaned into their hands to push them deeper in her ears.

    "She likes that," I said.

    "Well, she can't scratch with her back paws. I have to… do… it…" he grunted as he met her steady force.

    If the cover of her pillow needed washing, I threw it in the machine. If it held clothes, I tossed them in the dryer. If the dryer was full, I folded and stacked them neatly on top. If the floor around her required a mop, I used it on the whole downstairs. If there were dishes in the sink, I washed them.

I had nowhere else to be. Helping out in an acute situation had a refreshing quality for me. My own marriage hadn't ended with the snap of a spine, but after a four-year battle with the languid cancer of an affair. I was tired. And jaded. But the urgency of Fontana's care spawned a sense of importance in me and, with it, enough adrenaline to bring about a slight stirring in my mind, like the nearly imperceptible light that slowly brings about the hint of pre-dawn.

He noticed the few small things I did and found it remarkable that someone could care for him, as well as Fontana. "You've done more laundry here in the last month than she did the entire marriage," he observed. I noticed his gratitude and found it remarkable that someone would say thank you for such trifles. To me, I did so little compared to sacrifices I'd made before that had gone unnoticed.

As Fontana's fur began to grow back in over the healing scar, she figured out how to roll off of her pillow, how to drag her back half around, and eventually how to break out of her metal pen. As her strength grew, so did her resolve. I would fit my key into the door to find her pillow empty.

Then the boys would play hide-and-seek and we would search not only for Fontana, but also for her new accomplishments. "Mom! Come here! She made it through the dog door!" She lay basking in the sun like it was perfectly expected. Her fur was warm to my touch and the sunlight shone in her eyes.

One day we couldn't find her anywhere, inside or out. My youngest child, the devious one himself, discovered the clue: a bungee cord and wooden railing chewed to bits, allowing only the most stubborn of dogs to climb the staircase to the second floor. Unbelievably, she had not only conquered all that with the use of only two paws, but had also managed to climb atop his queen-sized bed, the very one she'd broken her back jumping off of. She looked comfortable and quite pleased.

I was terrified that she would hurt herself again. We'd clean up her various messes, reset and fortify her boundaries, and corral her again, but inside, I also marveled. Whatever contraptions we rigged up did not discourage her. She just tirelessly worked at them, first from one direction and then another until she got what she wanted. It made me consider what I wanted. What impediments had I let deter me from getting where I wanted to be? I considered perseverance... no... sheer stubbornness. I thought of the simple luxuries I let life keep me from: the warmth of the sun, the indulgence of a hard-earned nap in a soft, familiar bed.

One night I woke from a dream in which I had been with Fontana in the grass, running my hands down her flanks. In the darkness, I could still feel the tickle of her fur in my palms. I had not just been petting her; I had been pulling the sensation from the top of her body down her spine into her haunches. The nerves relit inside her as I coaxed the ability to feel back down her neural path. The healing, the way she and I made it happen together, was supernatural.

That afternoon, I tried it. I dug my fingers between her shoulder blades, massaging deeply as I traveled slowly downward, visualizing the nerve endings waking as if from a nap, stretching and tingling back into awareness. Every day, I did this, without looking for progress or acknowledging discouragement. I did it just as Fontana herself would have done. Just as she had taught us both to do.

He walked her with a harness that suspended her back legs while the front paddled around their morning loop. Slowly he lowered the sling so that her back paws began to bear a tiny bit of weight. I watched as his faith grew, like a muscle previously unused and then called into regular action, just as his bicep hardened under the sleeve of his sweatshirt as he carried her weight for her.

We watched together as the sunrises sprung from the Atlantic earlier and earlier and warmed into spring as her hips began to sway in coordination with her front legs. Though she still could not hold any weight, her back paws had begun to touch the ground and move in intentional steps.

We talked about Fontana as we walked. "At the vet yesterday, they squeezed the pad of each back paw. She yelped!" This was fantastic. I thought about what it was like to feel again, even if only pain. I thought about how life was a joy to experience, even when it hurt. Why are our hearts like this? Why do we cling so tenaciously to the experience, fully aware of the risk?

"The other day when I was petting her," I said, "she turned back and looked at me in surprise. She felt my hands in a place she didn't expect to feel." I remembered my dream and wondered if healing that deeply was possible. I wondered if it was foolish to hope for the ten percent chance of recovery she'd been given.

Fontana didn't wonder. She just kept demanding that her body do what it always had before and soon the reflexive movement of her hips was intentional and her paws didn't just touch the ground, but pushed off of it with increasing force. Soon we could prop her up and she would stand on all fours, her back gently swaying as she took over her balance. Day by day, she put the pieces together. Sunrise by sunrise we shared the joy of her recovery, tossing a stick or a ball and then watching her maneuver after it, giving her a hearty rub of approval when she returned. Occasionally, as our hands plowed through her soft, black fur, they would brush up against each other. And that was how we all healed, by pressing into the injured and abandoned spaces within.

I don't want to think that Fontana had to break her back to teach us all to feel and love and hope again, but I do know that the three of us came together at precisely the right moment to help each other through a very long and painful year at the end of which we each could—amazingly!—do very ordinary tasks.

Fontana could walk in spite of having broken her spine. He could open a heart to others that was once cruelly mishandled. I could love and hope around the memory of betrayal.

Every morning we walk, Fontana in front, only a slight and occasional limp indicating anything unusual, her eyes sparkling with equal parts morning sun and the playfully tenacious spirit that brought us all to this moment. And what is most amazing isn't amazing at all; it's perfectly normal. The miracles that led us here are hidden in our pockets like shells.

BUDDY
By Chuck Willman

my best friend weighs only 16 pounds,
has four bony little legs with pigeon-toed front paws,
and was rescued from a shelter at four months old,
found starving and abandoned in a city intersection.
he doesn't care that I'm a stick-figure of a man wasting away,
thanks to a disease making me invisible to humans.
he doesn't care that I snore loudly, or wake from demons
haunting me in the middle of the night, or that I toss and turn
the rest of the time because of pain in my crumbling body,
forcing him to uncurl himself from my side and re-curl himself
near my head, or jump down from the bed altogether
to find comfort on the sofa that still holds enough
of my scent for him to doze.
he doesn't care when I'm angry at the world,
or I sit crying when I'm afraid or too exhausted
to give a damn anymore, wondering how or when
a new struggle will begin, knowing one is always
lurking around the corner.
he only cares that he can stretch out in my bony lap,
sitting with me as if we've known each other
for more lives than we can count, never having to speak,
just listening to each other's breath and heartbeats.
he only cares that I scratch his head, rub his belly,
and let him lick my knees and hands while we
cuddle in front of the TV, and knowing that
wherever I go he can find me.
he only cares that I feed him, let him play with his
favorite stuffed toy that squeaks, even when I have
a migraine headache, take our short walks,
and pick him up when he's terrified of everything

blowing around him in the strong desert storms,
clinging to my side when there's lightning and thunder.
he only cares that I always come home after running errands,
his tail wagging so hard it could fly off his body,
and give him treats when he's good,
or even when he's been bad sometimes.
I only care that he loves me for who I am,
whatever mood I'm in, no matter what,
and that I know he'll be right by my side, looking at me
with the big brown eyes that swallow his little face,
reassuring me that everything's fine, for now.

TRANSITION
By Sandra Ervin Adams

After losing the house to foreclosure,
and moving to the mobile home,
I was in need of my rescued felines'
soothing balm.
One of the smaller ones, a Calico,
looked up at my room door, tilted
her head, blinked her eyes as if to say,
Mommy, please let me come in.
Now on sleepless nights, she stays
on my bed, and should tears
roll down my face, she is here
to blot them with soft paws.

SENSE OF COMFORT
By Carolyn T. Johnson

My calico cat
rests on my chest,
purrs, kneads,
soaks in my essence

Hand-chosen by Dad
before his untimely death,
she's the perfect prescription
for my lonely heart

Wiping fresh tear
drops from my cheeks,
I scratch between
her upturned ears

She lifts her feline head,
sniffs my damp hand,
then gently licks away
sorrow with her
sandpaper tongue

Her luminous green eyes
gaze into mine, as if
to say, *I know,*
I miss him too

DO NOT DELETE
By Deborah Schildkraut

The subject line in the email says: "Elderly corgi needs home."

"Delete it," your inner voice warns. You don't read the email, hoping you'll forget about it. But you don't delete it either.

You know what it's going to say. "Urgent. Elderly corgi needs home. If not adopted, will be euthanized in five days." Or four days or tomorrow. Always urgent.

"Dammit," you say aloud. "I don't need another dog." Who are you kidding? You need dogs like you need air. People annoy you and patience is not your virtue - except when it comes to dogs.

You move away from the computer and look in the foyer mirror. Yep, "Sucker" is still tattooed on your forehead.

Back at the desk, you open the email. "Urgent. 11-yr-old corgi needs home immediately. Owner in hospice care. Call Carrie for more information."

You write down the phone number and hide the slip of paper in your back pocket so you can pretend it isn't there. Ten minutes later you're punching Carrie's number into the phone.

She tells you about the corgi. He's a genuine curmudgeon, that Reggie, been looked after by hospice workers for almost two years. Fed, walked, watered but not much time for attention. He's a tough old guy, standoffish now, maybe even depressed.

You like challenges, you say.

Then Carrie tells you about Raymond. Raymond is dying from AIDS. He's had Reggie since he was a puppy. Raymond is not as concerned about dying as he is about what is going to happen to Reggie afterward. The dog is his best friend, soulmate, child. Raymond is consumed with worry. Carrie tells you she has tried for months to place Reggie but no one wants a grouchy, antisocial 11-year-old dog. She has promised Raymond she will try one last time. Raymond's time is measured in days. You are Reggie's last chance. She isn't consciously trying to guilt you into taking the dog, but she's doing a pretty good job.

Even though she doesn't ask, you tell Carrie about your qualifications. You're an experienced dog person and have a fondness for hard-luck cases. You have three dogs and a large back yard. You are trying to impress Carrie, though you realize that she would give Reggie to just about anybody right now.

"So you'll take Reggie?" she asks.

"Probably," you say, as if you had a choice.

The relief in her voice is apparent by a great exhalation of air, and she hurries off the phone before you change your mind.

Two days later, you're tooling up the interstate on your way to adopt a dog you haven't even met. You don't know if you'll like each other, or if he'll get along with the rest of your dogs. No matter. Raymond adores Reggie, and that's a good sign.

When you arrive, Carrie is waiting at the door. You sense immediately that something is wrong. She speaks in a hushed tone. Raymond died during the night.

Several people are milling about the house, waiting for Raymond's family to arrive. Reggie is curled up in a corner of the kitchen. He ignores you, his one last chance. Carrie has already packed his bag, eleven years of doggy possessions: bowl, leash, food, a baggie of treats, two squeaky toys and a pillow that belonged to Raymond. You try to coax the dog with a biscuit. But Reggie is above a bribe. He does not move.

Carrie says that Reggie's been lethargic all morning, and hopes he isn't getting sick. He is grieving you tell her and ask if he has been allowed to see Raymond. No one thought to do that. Raymond's body has not been removed, and you ask her to take Reggie to see him. He needs to see Raymond for closure, you explain. She seems to understand and doesn't look at you as if you're a nut case.

Reggie and Carrie disappear into Raymond's bedroom. When they come back to the kitchen, Reggie heads to the door and waits to be taken out. Carrie says that she placed Reggie on the bed with Raymond. The dog sniffed him from head to toe. Then Reggie lay beside his friend, the length of his furry body tight against Raymond's body. Eyes closed and head tucked in the crook of Raymond's arm, Reggie remained still for almost ten minutes before he stood and jumped off the bed.

Carrie hands you the leash and bag. She rubs Reggie's head as if it were a genie's lamp and wishes him well.

One thing you have to ask. "Did Raymond know that Reggie found a new home?"

"Yes," she replies. "He did."

Reggie hops into the truck on the floor of the passenger side. He curls up into a ball. The old truck purrs when you turn it on. Sam Cooke croons from the Oldies station and you sing along.

"*You you you you send me.*"

Reggie looks up from the floor.

"*Honest you, honest you do, honest you do.*"

Reggie jumps onto the front seat

"*At first I thought it was infatuation but woo it lasted so long.*"

He circles three times before he settles next to you. Not his head, mind you, but his furry little butt against your hip. You smile, but not so that Reggie can see.

"*Now I find myself wanting to marry you and take you home.*"

You have to chuckle, almost perfect lyrics for the occasion, except for the marrying part.

"*Whoa -oh -oh –oh- oh- oh.*" You're really crooning now.

You reach over to pat Reggie. He growls, but he doesn't move. You withdraw your hand. "Okay, pal. When you're ready," you tell him, "When you're ready."

A GENTLE HEALER
By Nikki Rosen

She was only forty pounds if that, but in my book, she was a pretty big hero. I brought Sasha home when she was six months old – a tiny bundle of white fluff. She stood a bit taller than a typical Bichon Frise, but her soft white coat, her gentle manner and her happy nature made her the best dog for our family. When she turned three years old, I started working out of the basement of our home, counseling women who struggled with issues related to child abuse and rape. Many of these women had difficulty speaking. They often sat in front me, on the edge of their seat, as if they were prepared to run out should they need to do so. Most looked uncomfortable and they frequently repeated they couldn't think of anything to say.

During one of these sessions, I became aware of Sasha standing on the top step peeking through the railing at us. My client hadn't noticed her and I had to fight to keep myself from laughing. I watched as she moved down a step and squeezed her head through the banister to peek out at me again. After a minute, she pulled her head back in and gingerly stepped down one more stair. I stood to my feet and sternly told her to go back upstairs. My client turned around and seeing the dog, begged me to let her come downstairs.

Nodding, I called Sasha to come to me. She happily scooted down the rest of the steps, ran and jumped into my lap. My client broke out in a huge smile and asked if she could hold her. I lifted my wiggling, excited pup onto her lap. The dog settled down, positioning her body so that she faced me. A few strands of wispy hair hung over her big brown eyes which seemed to be saying, *I can help this woman. I can help her talk.*

And that's exactly what she did. As the woman stroked the dog's soft white fur, something amazing happened. The client started to relax and then she began to talk. Over the next few years I had Sasha attend every counseling session. She proved her expertise in helping every client feel comfortable enough to tell their story.

My unlikely counseling partner taught me the therapeutic power of dogs in helping people who are damaged by abuse and trauma. She became the tool for their healing. Somehow, as the person preoccupied themselves with touching and stroking the dog, they were able to calm their fears and anxieties enough to disclose the shame and pain that had kept them stuck. And when they cried, Sasha instinctively pushed her head into their chests and even licked their tears away. Her unconditional acceptance and gentle support worked wonders.

The power of dogs to help people heal and recover from trauma is powerful. Their presence can make a huge difference in the person's ability to open up and let go enough to move forward in recovery.

I am grateful to have had the experience to co-partner with Sasha, making a difference in the lives of so many.

BAILEY: A GOLDEN RETRIEVER
By Paul Cummins

He loves retrieving balls,
That's his DNA and he
Would retrieve all day,
All night until he dropped
If you would keep throwing;
But that's not what defines him—
Any more than the affection
He craves and would receive
In endless tummy-rubs
As long as you would rub;
But that too is not defining—
Nor the tail-thumping if you
So much as look his way or say
His name, if ever so softly,
Soft, soft thump;
But that as well does not define.
No, it is his eyes—
A trace of sadness programmed perhaps
To say creatures like me are rare
And this world does not grasp
The essence of why we are here;
Eyes which combine wild and tame
In a sweetness so pure
That he fills the void;
And playing catch,
Tummy-rubbing and tail-thumping
Compel us to look into the world
Which lies behind his gentle eyes.

THE GIFT OF TEARS
By Alan Pratt

I was fifteen when my mother died, leaving behind five children and a husband who had no clue about what to do next. She had battled cancer for four years, lived two years longer than they said she would live, but still her death was a surprise.

She died at home, in her bed. On that September morning, after my father told us she was dead, I opened the bedroom door and walked inside. I saw her corpse, touched her hand. That cold touch has stayed with me forever.

Four months later, my grandfather, the adult I most trusted, the adult who always had time to listen to me, died in the hospital. He was a complicated man, an alcoholic who no longer drank, fiercely proud and independent, a physically short man who always felt the need to prove himself equal to any task.

I went to the hospital with my father. Going into my grandfather's hospital room to get his clothing, I saw my grandfather's corpse lying in the bed. My grandfather died of lung disease, his face frozen in his final struggle for breath. I still feel his last gasp.

At fifteen, trying to understand all this, I made what seemed a rational decision. If everyone I loved died, I would end the death by loving no one. I would, in the words of the Paul Simon song, become a rock, an island.

In a crowded family, with each member struggling with their own grief, my withdrawal from life went unnoticed. I was always the classic middle child, mostly invisible. Now no one noticed that I rarely spoke, never laughed, or cried. I was a shadow to everyone, except Ladybug.

Ladybug, known as Lady, was the ugliest little dog I have ever seen. It's hard to say what breeds were mixed up in her, but they were mixed up well. She had the mustache and goatee of a schnauzer, once brown but now largely white. Her coat, short and wiry, was mostly black, with longer white hairs sticking up here and there. She had short, thin black legs and white feet. She was a bit fat, because she had a regular treat route in the neighborhood. Each morning she would wander house to house in the neighborhood, sitting on back steps until the neighbors rewarded her with a treat.

She was a lady in every sense of the word. She did not play favorites. In a large family, she was truly "our" dog, equally loved and loving to all. In fact, she was to a large extent the neighborhood dog. Everyone loved Lady.

Did she change when she sensed my need, or did I change her without realizing what I was doing? I'll never know. I just know that as I withdrew deeper and deeper into my own world, Lady followed, and lead me back. She refused to allow me to turn my back on love.

There were days when Lady was the only one I spoke to. If I sat by myself, she joined me, resting her head on my lap, encouraging my hand to pet her head. I could not take a walk without her following. She became my dog.

The summer after my grandfather's death, Lady began showing signs of failing health. She was at least twelve years old, maybe older. We didn't know her age. She was the only dog any of us remembered. Her face was completely white now, spotted by her two small brown eyes and her wet black nose.

She died one summer evening on the sidewalk in front of our house. She had been chasing a ball, and simply collapsed, trembling. Someone — my brother? — called for me to come quickly. She died in my arms.

In her death, she gave me a final gift. The gift of tears. There on that sidewalk, in front of family and neighbors, I was finally able to cry and release my grief. They were tears for my mother, tears for my grandfather, and tears for the dog who had loved me when I most needed it. I didn't care who saw the tears. I cried.

We buried Lady in the back yard that night. I'm sure we all dug the grave, although I only remember digging it myself. We wrapped her in her favorite blanket and murmured some heartfelt prayers. We cried, the entire family, joined at last in shared grieving for the losses we had endured.

It has been over forty years since Lady's death. I have had many dogs, and even a few cats, in that time. I have lived a life worth living. My wife, my children and my grandchildren have all seen Lady's picture on my wall. They think she is just my first dog.

She was so much more. She was my light in the darkness, the one who loved me when I had given up on love, the one who sensed my need and filled it. I tear up when I think of her, tears of gratitude and wonder.

The gift of tears. That is what she gave me. Without her, I might never have cried, never felt again. That ugly little dog reached into the depths of my grief where I was hiding and brought me back to the living. The tears that are falling as I write this, nearly a half century later, are tears of joy for a dog who gave me back my life.

YOU MEAN THE WORLD TO ME
By Ruth Sabath Rosenthal

Clown-like happiest
On your back
Feet to the stars
Galactic capacity
To immerse in
Sensation
To stare into space
Entranced
As my fingers traverse
Your length and breadth
Your breath
Imperceptible
As though heaven bound
Till I stop stroking you
My precious dog

MIRACLE
By Lynn C. Johnston

If you had asked me five years ago what road my life would take, I never could have anticipated most of the events that ocurred. During this period, my always healthy mother was diagnosed with pancreatic cancer and succumbed to the disease seven months later. I was laid off from my job two months after the funeral. The next few years didn't get any better with only temporary job prospects and deepening financial woes.

I thought I had pretty much hit rock bottom. Then in the fall of 2009, my precious indoor Calico cat, Valentine, got outside and vanished.

Feeling like my nightmare was only getting worse, I was tormented with visions of all the horrible things she could encounter. Had she been injured by another animal or a car? Was she being held against her will? Was she getting enough food?

I plastered the neighborhood with flyers and knocked on nearly every door, meeting most of my neighbors for the first time. As I showed them her picture, their faces fell, often recalling their own agony of a lost pet. I asked that if they were religiously inclined to please keep Valentine's safe return in their prayers.

My teenage son and I roamed the neighborhood every night with flashlights, just hoping to catch a glimpse of her. And each night when we returned home unsuccessful, I was heartbroken. As the days dragged on, my hopes and faith were fading. I was crushed. It seemed as if God was kicking me when I was down.

But one night, three weeks to the day after she disappeared, my son announced that he heard her collar bell ringing outside. My heart leapt.

"Are you sure?" I said, too afraid to have my hopes dashed again.

"Yes, and I saw her. It was dark, but I'm sure it was her." He went on to say that she ran into the yard of the apartment building next door.

When he said that, I spontaneously broke into tears. I couldn't stop crying. She wasn't home yet, but at least I knew she was alive and healthy enough to run.

The next day we rented a humane animal trap from our local shelter, filled it with small chucks of Kentucky Fried Chicken (as they recommended), and prayed for a miracle. I slept on the living room sofa so I could be near our front door if the trap closed.

At three o'clock in the morning, my prayers were answered. Valentine was in the trap, filthy, scared, and about three pounds lighter than she left. I was never so happy to see her in my life.

I dropped to my knees and thanked God for bringing her home safely and bringing her light back into my life. It was a miracle.

That night, though Valentine, I learned two valuable lessons that have helped sustain me in times of crisis ever since: Miracles do happen and nightmares can have happy endings.

THE SEEING-EYE MAN
By Paul Sohar

Where do blind dogs want to go so badly? What is it they see when they cannot see? I often wonder when I take Maggie for a walk, holding the leash carefully away from myself so that this poor dog will not get entangled around my legs and I will not inadvertently kick her.

Yes, she is old and blind, yet just as eager to go walking as ever. Maybe it's an atavistic instinct to hunt that drives her to follow a scent I cannot smell, cannot even fathom its source. Actually, she was never a great hunter; like most domestic dogs she had very little of her wolf ancestors' ferocity.

In her younger days she would chase a cat or a squirrel, but she would not have known what to do if she had ever caught up with them. Now when I take her for a walk she displays the same eagerness to go; she would run if I let her. But where?

If life deprived me of my sight, I'd probably reject everything else it had to offer. I'd never get out of bed. That was what Maggie did for two weeks after her second eye, too, had gone completely blind. She just lay in a corner of the kitchen, refusing to eat or get up, responding neither to her name nor the aroma of her dish.

But two weeks later suddenly there she was, all over the kitchen, sniffing around, bumping into the feet of the table and ours too, but again barking happily when her name was called and ecstatically when she felt the leash being put on her. She had trouble negotiating the stoop steps, so at first I had to carry her out to the middle of the street. But once we were out there she picked her direction without hesitation and set out at a trot, or at a speed with which I could keep up. She seemed to be driven by the same old urgency of her younger days, but she still kept to the middle of the street, headed for a destination I could not see. I followed her blindly, so to speak, only watching out for occasional cars and salt-melted puddles that could have frozen her paws.

Now it's the same routine every evening. I just follow, trusting her tongue that points the way as she pants her grateful hymn to the solid pavement under her feet. I am subject to bouts of depression, a condition that renders me blind to my surroundings, to my life passing by. That's the time when it's best for me to take Maggie out for a walk and catch her spirit, her will to live, her ability to enjoy what she has -- and to forget about things she doesn't.

MY DOG IS SPIRITUAL AND ETERNAL
By Justin Blackburn

My dog is spiritual and eternal
He is small and yellow
He does not need a congregation
He likes to play, chew, tumble, wrestle and tug.
My dog is spiritual and eternal
He howls and barks
He does not need a Bible
He likes his snacks and blankets
My dog is spiritual and eternal
He wants to be petted and held
He does not need a religion
He likes to go to the park and leave puddles in the kitchen
My dog is spiritual and eternal
He let me teach him how to sit and do tricks
All he needs is himself
And I can feel God's everlasting presence

MISTIE'S MAGIC
By Beckie A. Miller

She was a young girl's first love. A buckskin, Quarter-horse mare with a dunn stripe down the middle of her back, long flowing mane and tail named Mistie. At least a long tail until the young girl, Christie, got hold of the scissors! A fourteen-year-old, gentle-giant; she was huge compared to my daughter's small stature at the age of ten years old.

It did not take long for me to learn that besides her gentle, loving nature, Mistie and my daughter had a very special bond. Their special bond would see the pair of them through some very tough times ahead, such as the loss of Christie's brother, Brian.

Mistie had a very protective sense about Christie and other children. This second-sense was apparent too with special adults. My disabled brother and sister, Stan and Cindy, came to visit and attend the graduation of Christie's brother, Brian, from high school. Because they both have Muscular Dystrophy, they had not been able to do many things in life, including, and up until this point, riding horses. We had total faith that Mistie would have the patience it would require for us to get them both, one at a time, on her back for a ride. It was a task requiring two strong men and a ladder to achieve the final moment, but the thrill in my sibling's eyes when they were atop a horse for the first time could not be measured by the work involved. Mistie understood this was a special situation and these adults were precious and fragile cargo.

Christie and Mistie joined 4-H and won first and second place ribbons consistently, even though Mistie was usually one of the oldest horses showing. Before Mistie came into my daughter's life, she only knew what a horse was. She had no previous experience, and my own was limited to riding a few times in high school because of dating a rodeo nut! Christie learned on her own and by watching others, but mostly it came naturally.

Unfortunately, with the advent of years and aging, Mistie developed acute leg problems. We placed her on the vet's suggested regimen of medications, and changed her shoeing to corrective with special padding to keep her more comfortable. This allowed them to have a few more years together. It was obvious that horse endured much discomfort to continue riding with her loving companion. Christie, knowing this, reluctantly began riding our other horse more often. Strawberry was a thoroughbred mix, whom we rescued from slaughter at six-months of age. Not that she did not love Strawberry and trained her totally from a young, wild filly, but she was not the same as Mistie.

A couple of years later, Mistie developed a uterine infection that our vet had been treating when her uterus gave out and ruptured. She died in a manner of minutes. Our vet, knowing how much Christie loved that horse went immediately to the high school to tell her personally, and bring her home to say goodbye. It literally broke her heart, but Christie had suffered much worse two years before, with the death of her brother, Brian. She was tough enough to handle it. I was the one who cried incessantly for the pain of loss my child had to endure again. Mistie was a big part of Christie's healing and coping with her brother's loss. The first weeks after his death she nearly rode Mistie to death herself. Riding was therapeutic for my daughter and Mistie understood this and endured pain herself to allow Christie to do so.

It is never easy saying goodbye to those we love and who hold a special place within our hearts. When you love someone this much how do you ever say goodbye? I believe the only way is in stages, and even then, I know we truly never say goodbye in our hearts. The spirit of any love shared remains with us forever, tucked safely alongside our priceless, precious memories. The lessons we learn from those who touch us so deeply, will remain with us throughout our lives. Christie will always treasure her special bond with her first love. She learned from Mistie the true meaning of friendship — trust and love. There will never be another Mistie as true magic cannot be repeated in exactly the same way, however, we can make room in our hearts for more magic once we heal.

I often enjoy reading the new book "craze" regarding near-death experiences and have noted many of them convey reports of seeing, not only loved ones who have previously died, but animal friends, too. I believe our non-human friends have a special place in heaven because they shared and gave so much of our love. Many moms, like my own, often console their children with the thought that their deceased pets are in heaven. Christie and Mistie have a special date in the distant future, and once again, they will ride new trails together and the magic of that special first love will be rekindled.

THE TIME OF HEALING
By Willard Stringham

I wasn't sure what to expect the first day I went to meet him. Twenty-six years ago my life was in a bad way all around, and I needed something to get me out of the miasma of continuing days, or I felt as if I might just slip away.

At the age of sixteen, I was sick more than I was well. And I don't just mean physically. A type of depression hung over me on an almost daily basis.

For years, I'd suffered various respiratory illnesses as a result of an immunological problem. At this particular time in my life, I began to attend home school just to recoup my health after a series of especially virulent illnesses.

If this wasn't enough to deal with, and believe me it was, a great deal of emotional turmoil came into my life as the result of a church my family attended and the school the church operated. I attended this school until I went to school at home.

Without getting into too many details, let's just say that the people I encountered here didn't appear to me to be too spiritually inclined. All of the nastiness that went on in my religious life left me doubting my faith. The experiences here didn't contribute to my life in any positive way.

My parents, and others, thought that I needed something to get me going again. I wanted to get a dog.

I was definitely lonely, and a dog would make an excellent companion. Dogs were the only animals I didn't test allergic to. The search began.

My search ended when I found a 1-year-old red and white Pembroke Welsh Corgi named Toby. When I first saw him, I knew without a shadow of doubt that he was the dog for me. With the transaction made, Toby became the newest member of the Stringham household.

After a sorting out period, Toby and I became fast friends. His presence and friendship chased away much of the loneliness and hurt I'd experienced. With his non-judgmental love always with me, Toby helped me to heal emotionally and feel that maybe I was worth something after all. He helped restore my faith. God must be good if he could bring something this good and positive into my life.

As I continued my home studies, my health improved steadily both physically and emotionally. But, it became apparent not long after Toby came to live with me that he had his own physical and emotional problems.

For months, Toby always shied away from feet as if he was afraid of someone kicking him. If a newspaper was picked up a room away the old boy immediately bolted to a hiding place. I felt terrible that anyone could mistreat such a wonderful, kind and friendly animal.

I made a special effort to always talk kindly to him and not raise my voice. I made sure that no one scared him and that he received much affection and praise.

After some time, Toby's fears slipped away one by one replaced by boldness, courage, and an overwhelming desire to watch out for my safety.

Unfortunately, just like me, Toby experienced health problems as well. Toby developed ulcerative colitis which tormented him throughout his life. I took him to countless veterinary appointments and feed him a plethora of pills. Thank God, Toby kept going and going in spite of the odds.

By taking care of Toby, I came out of myself and by each of us helping the other the pair of us together grew stronger.

I'm convinced that without each other, neither of us would have lasted too long in this world. Together we healed each other's wounds through love and friendship. The power of these two forces overcame the meanness that life tried to bring on us.

Toby and I were together for 12 years; 12 of the happiest years I can imagine. He's been gone from me many years now physically, but in spirit he's always with me reminding me of the power of love.

CATAPLEXY
By Cristina Ferrari-Logan

Swift and sweet
The furry feet
That across my stomach
Race.

Fluffy and soft
And high aloft
The tail that sweeps
My face.

Sometimes at night
We stage a fight
And she attacks
My toes.

Then she gives my book
Dismissive look,
Thus my reading
Must come to a close.

I wish I could say
It's been a pain-free day,
But that's okay.
She knows.

So I dim the light
And hold her tight
As we drift off
Nose to nose.

HEAVEN SENT
By Suzanne Manning

One hot Fourth of July weekend night, we had some company at our house here at the farm. A guest had come into the house letting me know that one of our dogs was out on the front porch. I looked at my two big Lab mixes that were already in the house, and knew it wasn't one of our dogs out there. They insisted, "There is a dog on your front porch and it looks like a big grizzly bear!" I went out to investigate, and sure enough, there was the big black shaggy dog resting on our porch. He wasn't bothering any of us, so I let him spend the night out there.

The next morning I called the dog officer and no one was in the office that weekend because of the holiday. This was no emergency, so we waited for the following Tuesday. Over the weekend, I had been feeding him, and we struck up a friendship. He would follow me all around the yard. He seemed to be a nice old boy just lost that's all.

Well, Tuesday came and I had finally gotten in touch with the Dog Officer. She was very busy and was not able to come pick him up at the time. She had already heard of the big black shaggy dog though, through recorded messages on her answering machine that she had received over the weekend from other people in our neighborhood. The dog had been going from house to house on our street, but no one else wanted him around so, they chased him off. The other neighbors had been calling her to come pick him up. We live on a farm and have many animals, he must have figured this was the place to be and settled in. The dog officer asked me if the dog trusted me enough so that I could give him a ride to the local shelter to drop him off. I agreed, and sure enough, he was happy to go for the ride in the car.

The dog officer said she would try to find his owner. She took out an ad in the local paper, in the Lost and Found. No one claimed him. I called all the shelters in the surrounding towns wondering if someone was missing their dog. No one claimed him.

My husband and I discussed the possibility of adopting him if no one were to come forward to claim him. My husband's reply was, "Absolutely not!" We had already taken in two goats and a pig from a divorce situation and he didn't want to take any more animals in. I reluctantly agreed and let it go.

Fourteen days had passed since I had seen that shaggy old boy, and I hadn't given it much thought, until the phone rang. It was the local shelter explaining that the fourteen days had passed and no one came forward to claim him. They explained to me that they had tried to muzzle him to give him a vaccine and he went crazy. They took this incident to be a sign of aggression, and found him to be unadoptable. I own the most lovable dog around, a Lab mix; he does not like to be muzzled at the vet. He reacts in the same way when you try to muzzle him, knocking tables and chairs over. I did not think this shaggy old boy was being aggressive at all, he was probably just scared. They explained further that his time was up, no one came forth to claim him and they could not keep him any longer he was going to be put-down.

Well my husband came home from work that night and went to go in the house as he always does, but he could not get the door open. Something was behind the door blocking it. Guess, who? You guessed it. It was the big old shaggy boy. He was lying in the back hall of his new home. I went and picked him up from the shelter and brought him home. I named him Romeo. He was a true love, love boy!

From that day forward on our trips around town, we would see the Dog Officer. Romeo would be in the front seat next to me in the car with his big head out the window. She would smile, and always say hi to him.

I had lost my brother when he was only 33 years old. My brother and I were very close. I had become very depressed after he died. Sometimes I would think to myself this dog appeared out of nowhere, no owner, no tags, or trace of anyone owning him. Where did he come from? I believe it was my brother, who sent him to me. Maybe that would sound completely ridiculous to someone else, but just knowing Romeo was around had brought me comfort and great peace. I had owned many animals in my lifetime but never had connected to any of them the way this dog and I connected. Romeo turned out to be a great companion. He and I spent many a night, him lying on the floor by the fire, and me sitting on the couch sipping my tea. He would have followed me to the ends of the earth.

He was not just a great companion to his human friends but the other animals on the farm as well. Our outdoor cats would lay in the sun with him right by his side. The cats would come running when they saw him outside and they would rub against him to greet him. Our indoor cats would knead at his shaggy fur and make a cozy bed within the fur of his belly I would find them sleeping together like that at night. He never even flinched as they did this to him. He never chased, or nipped at any of his feline friends.

We knew he was an older dog because we had taken him to the vet when we first brought him home. His teeth were worn, and he was aging quickly.

He had progressively gone deaf and his hind legs were giving out on him. Even on the days when he wasn't feeling well he would still follow me around the house from room to room. He let us know when it was his time to leave, so we took that unavoidable trip to the vet. I stayed right by his side the way he always stayed by mine. I knew he was deaf so I made sure we looked into each other's eyes, I thanked him, and I said good-bye. I knew in my heart, he was going home to be with my brother.

I said a little prayer and asked my brother to take good care of him.

His time on the farm was brief, four years, but he made lots of friends here, and really enjoyed the outdoors, and living on the farm. He was a true friend and he is greatly missed by all of us. Romeo had taught me one of life's most important lessons about loss.

Sometimes in life, someone will connect with you in a way that you will never forget as long as you live. The bond you share is like no other. When they are gone it truly leaves a void in your life, but you know you were truly blessed to have known them, and to have had them in your life no matter how brief.

My brother and Romeo were those two someones in my life...

A GREGORIAN KIND OF A CAT
By Elaine Morgan

"We all have a job to do in this house," I explain softly. "We all carry our weight around here. No one gets a free ride. The dogs upstairs guard the house and the property. I provide the food and the shelter for everybody. Your job is to catch mice. You have to earn your keep, too. Understand?"

As I take a rest on the old maroon crushed velvet sofa which was relegated to the basement last year, he lays across my chest with white sock paws folded over my heart in a prayerful posture. I wish the veterinarian could see him today. He's a shiny silver streak with splotches of white paint splattered on a compact, muscular feline frame. Undulating charcoal-colored stripes extend from the corner of each golden eye to the base of each gray-tipped ear.

He studies me through almond-shaped eyes, appearing to meditate on the meaning of each and every word that passes my lips. I wonder if he's reading me with his paws, interpreting the rumble of vibrations emanating from my chest, and translating the echoes into a silent language in his own mind in order to understand what I'm saying.

I told her he wasn't a charity case. I was willing to pay cash money for her to diagnose his injuries after he was hit by the car. After a thorough examination, she gave me her evaluation. She said he had a concussion and that he was badly bruised. Also, that he had an infestation of tape worms and ear mites.

Then she gave me her opinion, which I didn't ask for. She said he had a scruffy coat, that he was plain-looking, didn't purr, and he obviously had no personality. She said he didn't "talk" much either, and that he was either a barn cat or a stray. Then she went on to say he was unadoptable and that it would be wise to take him over to the S.P.C.A. I told her we both knew the S.P.C.A. would euthanize him in the condition he was in. She countered by saying it was kinder than putting him back on the road where I found him. I detected a smirk when she said he didn't even know how to cross a four-lane highway. I decided to take him home with me and put him in the basement to see what happened after he healed. Take it a day at a time before making a drastic decision. I wanted to give him a chance for adoption at the S.P.C.A. She sneered, saying he would spray my basement because he wasn't altered and he didn't know how to use a litter box either.

Doggedly, I told her we would see about that. Then I gave her my best "sing-song" version of my history of living with cats for years and my certainty that how he turned out depended on what kind of temperament he had. That I needed time to discern whether he was a lover, a hunter or a warrior. I assured the Veterinarian there had to be some kind of personality lurking under that dirty gray and white fur. She sniffed. I left with the cat.

My reverie is interrupted by the pleasant, monotone song emanating from the throat of the cat. Unable to think of a proper name for him, I continue to call him "Little Man." It seems to suit him, and he responds. A plain name for a plain-looking cat who sings in plainsong, I think to myself.

I complain about my aches and pains, and grumble about not having enough energy to do all of the things I want to do. I give him the weather report for the following day: Hot, hazy and humid. I also tell him what my itinerary is for tomorrow. He's quiet, except for the continual purring. I notice he's a good listener and he seems to smile a lot.

I ask him where he comes from. He doesn't answer. I say, "Okay. We'll simply leave the question and forget about finding the answer. That's probably what it's all about anyway. There are no guarantees in life that every relationship has to have full disclosure. Maybe it's the essence of the unfolding process of a relationship that is more important than the history or the outcome of it." I begin to wonder where the seduction actually began.

It took ten days. Ten days of climbing up and down the mountain of steep steps to and from the basement, leaving fresh food and thinking I was talking to an invisible cat. Then I finally felt a whisper of gray satin caress the calves of my legs. I chuckled as I realized I would eventually win him over. I knew it was best to continue to ignore him for the time being. I didn't want another cat anyway. When the last of my pampered feline family pets died, whose companionship I loved and cherished over many years, I decided not to get another cat. I still had the dogs. They were enough. Or where they?

On the eleventh day, I felt the tapping of soft paws on my sandals as I passed the oak desk and he darted out from the inside of the kneehole. I muttered to myself something about the possibility of my falling and breaking a hip or a leg if the cat tripped me up as I was passing by. The S.P.C.A. crossed my mind again.

His campaign strategy escalated to stretching the upper part of his torso, arching his back and rubbing my knees with both sides of his face. The next step in the seduction process was "spinning tales" with silver threads between my ankles and the calves of my legs. The following day he jumped onto the adjoining cushion as I sat and rested on the sofa. That night, he slid onto my lap.

I knew the psychological process was over when he stood on his hind legs with a front paw on each one of my shoulders. He inspected my nose with his own pink muzzle, and he proceeded to stroke both sides of my face with his cheeks. Nice cat, I thought: a lover by temperament, and one with an attitude of gratitude.

I pet his silver head and back. The timbre of his purring seems to intensify with each stroke of my hand. I close my eyes and relax as I listen to his plainsong, and I seem to be seeing through stained glass windows. Emerald green hills roll as far as my eye can see. Helicopter-like seeds drop from nodding fuchsia-colored thistle in a field of wildflowers. They glide slowly, without purpose or intention to the bank of a gurgling river. It opens its mouth and showers diamonds in the plainchant in the air.

I awaken refreshed from my nap. The vibration of his purring intensifies when I open my eyes. I tell him it's all about those nuances in between the start-up and the finish line. Then I go silent again as my heart and my head follow the music of the plainchant of his purr. After a few years of being without a cat in my life, I'm again appreciating the wisdom and stillness of the feline species. I'm once again relaxing to the chanson of a cat, thanks to "Little Man."

I feel my mind and emotions becoming still, and I'm about to surrender to the notion of tranquility. Then I feel myself gliding back to the banks of a river which gurgles diamonds in the air. I open one eye to soliloquize once more time. I say, "Little Man, did anybody ever tell you that you're a Gregorian kind of a cat? And, don't let me forget to tell the veterinarian she was wrong."

I start to fall asleep again, following the river and the celebration of the liturgy in the air.

ISIS
By Mark McGuire-Schwartz

At 3 am she's caught a mouse. She wakes me
With muted calls. It does not sound like her.
Is she sick? Perhaps it is another cat, outside.
When I find her, there is something in her mouth.
She places it on the carpet, and I capture it in a can.

How proud I am that she has presented me this gift:
Live, unharmed. That she thought to wake me. To share
Her triumph. The reflexes are still there.

The next morning she wakes me again. 6:35 am,
This time. No mouse. Just purring. She has walked up
My legs, and is sitting on my chest, purring.

A PLACE IN THE HEART
By Scott Peterson

I have a pair of hands that don't always work the way I want them to. When I pick up a paint brush, for example, as much paint ends up on me as the wall, and the shelves of the bookcases I build for my daughters' rooms are noticeably slanted no matter how meticulously I use my level and saw. The simple task of replacing an ordinary lock on a shed door becomes a major ordeal before my stubby little fingers can coax them together. I have a reverse Midas touch, it seems - whatever I handle comes out a little more crooked, a little more bent, a little more out of kilter then they were before.

There is one area, however, where my hard to manage fingers never failed, and that was with my little cat Poco. One stroke of my index finger, moving up from the tip of her nose, between her ears, and along her back to her tail was enough to throw her into a ferocious fit of purring. This is what I liked best about her, this unquestioned, unqualified acceptance of my presence as a positive force in her life. My life, like all others, is not always a placid journey. As hard as it is for me to comprehend, my family is not always pleased with my behavior. My wife barely tolerates my attempts to keep the appliances and house running smoothly, and the piles of paper that build up on my desk like drifts of snow in January drive her into fits of exasperation. Likewise, my teenage daughters do not always appreciate my input into their lives, especially when I have to play the role of stern father. Poco, though, accepted whatever I had to offer, even a little stroke from these inept fingers, and turned it into something good in her life.

Just opening the basement door and letting her back into the world each morning was enough to send her into the highest levels of ecstasy. Poco would pop through the door like a cork off a champagne bottle, weaving around my ankles and defying death from being flattened by my size eleven feet. Together we would move to the kitchen table, locked into this little cat-dance, and she would be in my lap before

I could settle in my chair for my morning coffee. She would push her head against my fingers as I rubbed the space between her ears, breaking into a ferocious fit of purring, her body rattling and shaking, stirring up little ripples of vibrations in the coffee cup sitting on the table. Often her long tail would flick up into the air and she would be on it like a hunk of raw fish, batting it around and chomping on the tip until it would slowly dawn on her that she was chewing on something attached to her own body, and I would have to massage her ears until she began purring once again.

Bringing forth so much happiness in another living thing is good for our souls. Our lives become larger and more purposeful when we commit to something beyond our own selves, even if it is only to an oddball little cat. We give a piece of ourselves away, merge with another living thing, and in return, become something larger. To serve someone else, for no tangible gain in return, caters to our better sides and make us more humane and compassionate people.

Anyway, it wasn't a big surprise when my wife called me at my office one day and informed me that our neighbors had found Poco by the side of the road. My cat had too much energy, too much spirit and curiosity to serve out her time as a house cat. She spent her days roaming the fields around our house chasing butterflies and hunting down rodents like the lion she longed to be before returning home to spend to her time pursuing the perfect lap for her evening nap. This time, however, she didn't make it all the way home.

Still, I felt a small piece of my heart chip off when I heard the news, and another when I came home and buried her in our garden where she loved pestering the insects and other flying creatures. Nothing big, though. It was only a cat, after all. The little pieces would heal, and the memories would fade into a faint glow in a distant corner of my mind quickly enough.

The memories haven't faded, though. And those pieces of my heart - they haven't filled, either. Funny, but I always thought I was taking care of Poco, fulfilling her needs and making her happy. As it turns out, though, she was passing back to me just as much as I was giving to her. What I thought was a one way street was actually a busy two-lane highway, and after she was gone she followed that highway right into my heart.

And now that she's there, she is welcome to stay as long as she wants. It feels kind of nice with her hanging around, and after all, considering how much she has given to me, it's the very least I can do.

BLACK DOG
for Shadow, Angel, and Sue...
By Wendy Wolf

There's a trail where I walk,
a wide, flat, gravel path.
There are trees and scrub on either side;
beyond that, a farm and a trailer park;
beyond that, mountains, alive with mist.
In the autumn,
fat, red-gold apples fall from messy branches.
In the summer,
purple-black berries burst from tangled vines.
I pass a woman on the trail
pushing an empty stroller.
A big canvas stroller,
with a cushion inside,
very low to the ground,
like a hollowed out egg.
She's with two dogs—
one runs ahead,
brown and white and spry;
the other one follows,
woolly and black,
with thick legs, a short snout.
He looks like a bear.
I laugh and tell her so.
She smiles at me,
and says, "I know."
After I pass them, I turn around.
I notice the black dog
moves painfully slowly
on stiff, crooked legs.

The trail is a loop.
We cross paths again.
And now I know what the stroller is for —
the black dog is inside.
My chest is constricted;
there are tears in my eyes,
and I think to myself,
that's what love looks like.

CALYPSO
By Holly Day

she's still unfamiliar, not sure
of the longer hair, the gray
where I was used to short, plush gold
but she's comfortable. her purr
heals my hands
just the same.

I'm still not sure
she wants to be here, more than a roof
and a bowl of food and water
but she hasn't tried to leave yet.
and she sleeps in my bed
just the same.

she is not a reflection of me
doesn't share my fear of loud noises
and strangers — she is still a stranger.
but she curls up in my lap and
purrs straight through my bones
just the same.

LADY'S LOYALTY
By Glenda Barrett

    This morning in the daily paper, I notice the words, "COLLIE FOR SALE." As I look at the picture, it brings back memories of a collie I once knew. At the time, I was working as a home health aide and traveling from home to home in North Georgia taking care of the elderly.

    It was not an easy job, but a rewarding one. It left me many memories and this one has stayed with me.

    I remember vividly the first time I met Millie. She was sitting in a rocking chair, and close to the side of the chair sat Lady, a miniature collie with beautiful markings. I found out later she had been a show dog at one time. As I walked over and introduced myself, Millie held out her tiny, frail hand to greet me. She was very petite and delicate looking and wore a white turban on her head.

    Being an animal lover myself, I spoke a few words to Lady as well. By her low growl and high, shrill bark, it was evident that she did not want any part of me. She made it plain from the start that her job was to guard her master, and she did it well. I figured I'd win the dog over in no time because I usually had a way with dogs, but I soon found nothing I did eased Lady's anxiety.

    My job was to help bathe Millie on my visits, and she was very cooperative. At first she was quite reserved, but as time went on she began to trust and confide in me more, even telling me about her brain cancer and the loss of her hair. Some days she was not up to conversation, so I followed her lead. I noticed that she lived alone, except for Lady, and I didn't notice any visitors.

    As Millie's condition worsened, I was required to see her more often. When she became unable to walk to the bathroom, I gave her bed baths instead of helping her to the tub. As I bathed Millie, Lady positioned herself in the bed on the other side of Millie, and kept a strict eye on me the whole time I worked. Each time I talked to Lady as well, but it made no difference, she loved Millie and that was her main concern.

Millie felt the same way about Lady; there was a deep bond between them and a mutual understanding. Lady seemed to be all she had.

After several baths, Lady did seem to relax some, but she still kept up her guard. At least her barking and growling had stopped, I could be thankful for that.

One Monday when I walked in to the office to get my schedule, I received the shocking news. Millie had passed away over the weekend. I was amazed at the loss I felt. I had become attached to her and Lady.

In the challenge to get to know them both, I had become involved emotionally. A few weeks later I received a phone call from Millie's daughter. She was interested in finding a home for Lady and wondered if I would like to have her. Because of my allergies I felt I had to refuse. I explained to her I would try to find a home for Lady though. In a few days, I was lucky to find a nurse who was willing to take her.

A couple of months went by before I saw the nurse again and got the opportunity to ask about Lady. When I asked how she was doing, the nurse sadly informed me that Lady only lived a couple of months after her owner passed away.

She muttered something about, "Maybe, she got into some kind of poison or something." Again, I felt some sadness, but somehow I wasn't surprised to hear the news. I'd seen firsthand the strong bond between the two, and I'd often wondered how Lady would cope without her Master. I had my own theory. It was obvious to me one couldn't live without the other. They simply had to be together.

FIERCE ATTACHMENT
By Tina Traster

I put a cup of hot tea on the wood table. I wanted the small sofa to take me in its arms and cocoon me. The low November sunlight trickled through the window. Just as I kicked off my shoes I noticed his head strained forward. I thought he'd cough up a hairball. He didn't. His body remained pinched, fixed tight in a crouched posture. I waited. Waited for him to relax into the graceful U shape he usually assumes when he reclines on the rug.

Time froze. He remained motionless. I got closer, crouching like a cautious animal. His lips were slightly apart; his neck puffing at regular intervals as he drew in each strained breath. I massaged under his throat. My heart rate accelerated.

I know what can happen when you rush your animal to the emergency room.

With each passing moment I said, "Breathe normal, breathe normal." I knew each breath could be his last. I stopped pleading and yanked the cat box from the closet, shoes and paper bags raining down on me. I didn't close the closet door. He walked into the box without a fight.

"My cat can't breathe," I screamed when I arrived at the animal hospital.

The attendant in scrubs lifted the box from me and whisked him through wood doors with glass transoms. I rose on my toes to see what I could see through the glass. I couldn't see him. I wanted to be there to comfort him. In that moment of pandemonium I thought about my dog Chelsea; how I had not been there at the end. How when it came time to play God and administer relief from suffering I lay in bed wailing, the way I imagine a soldier's wife does when the man with the telegram leaves. I lay in bed that night writhing in a pain so searing I couldn't see or breathe. I had kissed him good-bye and my husband lifted him into his arms and took him into the living room. There he met the doctor. I covered my ears because I didn't want any last sound to remember. When my husband returned to the bedroom, he handed me a lock of his silky hair. That was 10 years ago. When I conjure it, or it catches up to me, it is five minutes ago and I am raw and unprotected from the shock of loss and finality.

"We've put your cat in oxygen," the doctor told me when she came out of the room.

My knees buckled and I dropped hard onto the metal chair, the television blaring overhead. "Oxygen," I asked, obviously frightened.

We need to take a chest X-ray to see what's going on. Can you sign here?"

"What's wrong with him," I cried.

"He's wheezing. There's some congestion in his lungs. I don't see anything lodged in his throat. I think we should take an X-ray. I suspect it may be kitty asthma."

I nodded. I signed the paper. I remembered that awful night when Chelsea was put in an oxygen tank. How the young night-shift attendant assured me he wasn't dying. But he was. He had a rare cancerous tumor in his nose. He was gone in six weeks. He had been the only warmth I'd known in the final years of a cold marriage. He was the child I never had with my first husband. His death was the first death that mattered. I lost a piece of my heart the day the gravediggers lowered his little pine coffin into the hole of dirt on the hillside at Hartsdale Cemetery.

I kept pulling out my cell phone to look at the time. I told myself this is an eight-year-old cat who seems perfectly healthy but my fears possessed the skill of a swordsman, knowing exactly where to pierce. I stretched the neck of my turtleneck. I couldn't bear to chat with the woman with the perky dog so I avoided her eye. My breath was as shallow as a pool of summer rain.

The doctor returned with her best guesses. The oxygen was working. His breathing was less labored. The X-rays showed minor congestion. "Kitty asthma" she said. She recommends a steroid to reduce inflammation. She said he might need to stay overnight and my legs went flaccid.

"Overnight?" I asked.

"Why?"

"Just to keep him under observation."

"But if he's breathing normally, why does he need to be here overnight?"

"Well, Ms. Traster, maybe he doesn't. We just need to watch him hour by hour to see how long it takes for his breathing rate to return to normal."

Ten days before Chelsea died I went to Brooklyn to claim the last remnants from my childhood house. My parents were moving. It was a chill December day, the kind you remember for its steel sky and the taste of snow in the air. My husband and I got out of the car. As I stood in the driveway, looking at the old house, something darted across my ankles so fast I didn't at first realize it was a palm-size kitten. He walked to a puddle of dirty water and lapped at it. I bent down on one knee and draped my hand along his tiny torso. He was black and white. When he sat on his haunches he looked like a perfect piece of porcelain. I had never before lived with a cat. I looked up at my husband and said, "Go inside and tell my mother to give you a cardboard box."

He wasn't more than six weeks. I remember nothing about his first ten days in our apartment because I was on a death watch for my dog. Every moment I prayed my dog would eat or drink or die naturally so I wouldn't have to make the decision that, to this day, I still consider the hardest of my life.

The day after Chelsea's death my husband said the vet, when leaving the apartment, suggested we close the windows. "The kitten could fall out and die," my husband recounted. I must have lowered the windows but I don't remember anything much at all. The days following my dog's death blurred from light to darkness with no distinction. The morning after his death I emptied bottles of pills that were supposed to save him, or at least buy him time. I screamed at the doctor. I picked up food and water bowls and threw them hard into the garbage. The weight of the clay sucked in the plastic garbage bag, collapsing in over itself. I collapsed on the hard kitchen floor.

I'd never known such despair, never. When my elderly grandmother died three years earlier, I was prepared. The suddenness of my baby's death left me feeling vacated from my body. Nothing felt hot or cold. I neither felt awake or asleep. I didn't absorb words I read. Food had no taste.

One night I was lying prone in bed. I felt pressure on my ankles. Then on my shin, thighs and my belly. This little cat was no longer willing to remain anonymous. He walked along my torso, continued up to my neck, leaned in to my nose and planted a kiss. I felt as though an angel gifted me with life. That kitten woke me from a deep slumber. He needed me. Not that my husband didn't. But I believed, as one might do in an effort to confront death, my dog's spirit returned to me through this cat.

It was with this awakening that I came to love this cat beyond measure. When he curls up against me, it looks like a mother breast-feeding.

"Floopy's your favorite cat," my husband teases me.

"Sshh," I say, holding a finger in front of my lips. "I love all five of them equally."

Everyone knows that's a lie. This cat saved my life.

That night, the vet called at 8 pm and said the cat was breathing fine. "You can come pick him up at 9," she said. "I think he'd be better off sleeping at home tonight with his mommy."

Obviously this veterinarian was a skilled psychologist.

FELINE THERAPY
By Sandra Ervin Adams

Lying in bed one chilly fall morning,
hoping to fall back asleep.
My lower back and legs in spasms,
cold although I turn the heat up.
My cat, a Siamese-mix, cries
at my room door until I let him in.
Once on my bed, he pounces upon
my feet, claws connected to covers,
then finally retracted.
He curls up next to me, his warm body
comforts, calms my pain.

STATE FAIR
By Paula Timpson

At three,
a little monkey
kissed me!
He played a wind-up accordion and as I
walked
through the Danbury State Fair with my family,
he reached out
to kiss my cheek;
a moment in time
I won't ever forget
the 'Angel ' monkey
who gently
blessed me
with
pure
Joy!

FLETCHER
By Barbara Moe

The caller ID announced our son Dan. He didn't call often. Was something wrong? Now in his early forties, he had a wife, three boys, and a dog. "Hi, Mom," he said. "I have a small favor to ask—actually a big one. Is there any way you could watch Fletcher for a week? We're taking the family to Mexico for Spring Break."

A week? Excuses, lots of them, came to mind. I'm busy. I'm not as young as I used to be. We haven't had a dog for a year, not since Angel died at age sixteen. I'm permanently retired from dog care. I don't like retrieving slobber-covered tennis balls. And I can already see black hairs on my white sweater.

Fletcher's a ten-year-old Lab who, in spite of his gray moustache, thinks he's a puppy—undisciplined and overly friendly. Besides, he has gastrointestinal issues.

Dan and his family inherited Fletcher from our daughter's family, who had fallen on hard times. Economic conditions had forced them to sell their condo and move to an apartment. NO DOGS ALLOWED. Dan and his wife worked overtime at their jobs; with three kids they had zero time for leisure. For their own preservation, they needed a vacation, a vacation from Fletcher.

"Mom?" Dan said. "Are you still there?"

"I'm here," I said, forcing cheer. "Sure. I'd love to take care of Fletcher." It would be me because my husband was leaving town for the targeted week.

I had seven days to get ready. In preparation, I visited the expensive neighborhood pet specialty store, the one with the homemade dog cookies. For the gastrointestinal issues the owner advised high nutrient dog food made with lamb and oatmeal. She also recommended probiotic powder, Pepto-Bismol, once-a-day feedings, and no table food. After racking up enough charges to keep the store in business for a few months, I went home and covered the basement floor with newspapers, the futon with old bedspreads. I was as ready as I'd ever be.

I persuaded myself this would be fun. Lots of walks, breathing fresh air—a girl and her dog.

On the appointed day, Fletcher jumped out of the minivan, tail wagging. Dan dumped the leash, dog bed, water dish, and more food at the back door. He rubbed Fletcher behind the ears, and the dog responded with a slobbery hand-lick. "Gotta run," Dan said and gave me a hug. "Thanks a lot!"

"Wait," I said. "If I have trouble, can I call your cell phone?"

"Call the vet." He waved and smiled as he backed out of the driveway.

The next morning, I sprang out of bed pre-alarm. 6 a.m. I'd been wrestling with a disturbing dream involving Fletcher's disappearance at the hands of hooded members of a dog cartel who had requested $5,000 ransom in dollar bills. It had been a restless night.

But now reality had asserted itself. "I'm coming, Fletcher." I'd almost forgotten my responsibilities to my mutt and his potential GI problems. Foregoing my usual shower and other morning preparations, I raced downstairs. What if the dognappers had pried open the back door? What if Fletcher had had an "accident." Fantasy and reality collided.

But neither had occurred. Fletcher stood on the landing, tail thumping on the wooden door like a metronome. A great watchdog, he barked when strangers approached the house but also when family arrived.

Get leash. Find plastic bags. I checked the outside. What looked like a foot of snow covered the newly sprouted daffodils and tulips. Find boots. Finally, "I'm ready, Fletcher."

As we left the house, an over-the-shoulder glance revealed no puddles or poops inside. Fletcher tugged, and I slipped on a patch of ice. Down I went. Right outside my own back door.

Getting up, brushing off flakes, I pushed the button on the retractable leash, which refused to retract. Yesterday I'd noticed on the handle a warning about the possibility of amputated fingers. I wondered if I'd have to run home with the non-retractable leash caught in my bloody stumps. How would I find my severed fingers in all this snow?

After two blocks, Fletcher assumed the dog-crouch stance and released the results of the oatmeal/lamb diet. As I stooped to do my work, Fletcher kicked wet snow into my face, then tried to lick it off. His gift to the world was so abundant, it filled two newspaper bags. I needed a third. What will dog owners do, I wondered, after the demise of the newspaper?

On our way again. Tail wagging, Fletcher approached Robin, a huge Irish setter, and Robin's owner Susan. Fletcher had never met a dog he didn't like and after rubbing noses, the dogs began a spirited tussle that tangled up the leashes. As soon as possible, I pulled Fletcher away, and observed the empty state of the third newspaper bag; the bottom had fallen out. "Oh, no," I said. We'd defaced the white snow. Retracing our steps, we found nothing.

At home, as I prepared to unzip my Salvation Army coat, I noticed brown smudges on my jeans. Yikes--on my gloves, too.

But wait. My coat zipper had jammed. I couldn't get the smelly thing off. My arms hung like peeled banana skins at my sides. I could not go on. I couldn't cope. Finally, I wiggled out, and the coat dropped to the floor with a thud. This was not fun; this was hell. Would I ever learn to say no? Tomorrow I'd have to put the dog in a kennel.

That afternoon I took Fletcher on his fourth walk of the day. Many walks, I reasoned, would prevent indoor accidents. But before I could steer him in a different direction, he had plunged his whole face into a snow bank. His long black tail thrashed in the frosty air. I tugged on the leash to no avail. He continued to dig, finally resurfacing with a large item clenched in his teeth. A chicken bone? A tuna sandwich? A poisoned bagel? I stuck my fingers in his mouth between his teeth in an effort to pry out the offending object. No luck. He wolfed it down.

Finally, home again. The furnace cranked out heat as I relaxed at my basement computer. Lying at my feet, Fletcher relaxed, too. Out of the corner of my eye, I glanced at him; he looked at me. His obsidian eyes radiated pleasure. He blinked and let out a huge sigh. Then he rested his head on his paws. Such a sweet dog. "What are you thinking, Fletcher?" He turned over for a tummy rub.

Maybe I wouldn't take Fletcher to the kennel after all. I got up to open the window a crack. My pet followed me to the corner of the room, where I discovered a pile of throw up. The chicken bone? Before dashing to the kitchen for paper towels, and perhaps a homemade dog cookie, I gave his head a pat. "Don't worry, Fletcher. It's all part of being a dog."

Five days later when Dan called about picking up Fletcher, I heard myself saying, "Hey, we were just getting acquainted. Could he stay another week?"

PUPPY LOVE
By Madana Dookieram

Knowing my distress, you come
With your puppy smile and all
Not knowing the horrible day I had

Nudging me for attention
Barking non stop
Welcoming me home with a smile of play
All you care about
Is I am home to play

You and your fun
Take my heart away
I watch you sleep
With your nose and tongue
Sticking out from beneath my bed
You don't care about what other people said
As long, as you have the safety of beneath my bed
Where you sleep and sleep all day long

Thank you, my sweet friend
For the puppy love
My old friend
So sweet and so kind
Unable to turn a blind eye
You love me for me
Or my bed
Who knows, I guess
But all you care about at the end of the day
Is that I am home with you,
Playing your silly puppy games

ALL DOGS DO GO TO HEAVEN
By Tammy P. Stafford

    Nancy is my friend and she is a dog lover. She is an extreme dog lover! She has four Great Danes that live with her and her husband in their home. Nancy has been my friend for over twenty years and for over twenty years she has been encouraging me to get a dog. She assured me a dog would help me love more, remove stress, and help me to generally feel better all over. But, I have a dog. I have two dogs, Percy and Tippy, both mutts, and I loved them or at least I thought I did.

    Nancy is the kind of pet owner that takes her dogs to the vet, a lot. If they need anything, she gets it for them. She takes them to doggie daycare, she takes them to the groomer, she takes them to the park, she walks them, she buys them gourmet dog food and she takes them to the acupuncturist. You get the picture. Nancy loves, with a capital L, her dogs. She will do anything for these animals similar to the way I care for my children. On the contrary, I love my dogs. I feed them, most of the time. I play with them by barely touching their heads and saying their names on my way from my garage to my front door. They get a bath if they stand outside in the rain. When they get sick, I watch them eat grass in my yard and hope they will get better. I love my dogs.

    I enjoy teasing Nancy when she talks about the care she gives her dogs and of course, how her dogs love her in return. Nancy and I have many things in common and we have many uncommon. I suppose the least common thing about Nancy and me is that she was raised Catholic and I was raised independent Southern Baptist. Now, I've said a mouth full and that's probably one of the greatest divides known to two women. Other than that one fact, Nancy and I are very similar individuals. We are brunettes (when Nancy isn't playing with her hair color), we are fair-skinned, not sun lovers, health-conscious, intelligent, talk with an accent (hers northern and mine southern), love the arts, love our families and our dogs.

Our relationship started as business and grew into true friendship despite our religious opinions. She was a salesperson and I, a buyer in business, but in friendship, we were two souls that shared like passions and convictions excepting one thing. She believed, just like the movie says, all dogs go to heaven. I believed that dogs, all animals, are soul-less and don't go anywhere when they die, especially not to heaven! I don't let dogs in my house, why would I want dogs in heaven with me? Many people don't like dogs and heaven is a place for people, not animals. Nancy and I had this discussion on several occasions with neither of us agreeing with the other.

It was a Thursday and Nancy was having a particularly hard day when she paid me a visit at my office. She began to explain to me that her dog, Tramp, was going to have to be put down and her husband had taken him to the vet, just that morning. I could sense and see the pain in Nancy's eyes as she struggled to choke back her tears while telling me about her pet. I didn't have a mirror in my office but I'm sure if you had taken a picture of me, I looked like a pompous peacock with my feathers spread in an elegant array and she predicted what I was thinking. She said, with a condemning voice, "Don't tell me Tramp won't go to doggie heaven, because I'm not listening!"

I didn't want to hurt my friend's feelings but at the same time, I can't back down on my staunch religious beliefs. I said to her, as kindly as possible, "I'm really sorry about Tramp, but, no, I don't think he will go to heaven." Nancy's countenance fell even more and this is one of those times when I wish I could have "found a little gray" as my husband calls it. My husband is forever telling me that I should not always be so "black and white" but a bit gray. At this point, I think my husband means well and I understand what he is saying. He wants me to soften a situation, not be so abrasive with my views, give a little understanding and so on, but he hasn't experienced the religious convictions that I have and I think he needs to be more "black and white," tell it like it is, stand on the promises, hell is hot and so on.

Nancy's dog did get put down that day and she immediately starting looking for a replacement. A replacement is what I called it; another member of the family is what Nancy saw it as because there would never be a replacement for Tramp, only another pet that filled the void that he had left behind. This was all very odd and unusual to me until my dog Tippy started coughing.

Tippy, a very active, small black and white female, would run a while and then have to stop to hack. Her activities slowed and her hacking grew worse. My husband and children insisted we take her to the doctor and she was diagnosed with congestive heart failure. She was prescribed medicine to help her breathe more freely by removing the fluid from around her heart and we took her home. My dad had rescued

Tippy from an abusive situation and she had been our pet for about five years. She was a very friendly dog that loved women and was very leery of the male species. We had her spayed and I told her all the time that I knew she must think she had died and gone to heaven because of the way she was treated before compared to the way she was living now. She always kind of grinned and showed me her teeth when I said that.

Percy, my other dog of 15 years, was a Chow mixture with a large plummy tail we got as a puppy. He had the sweetest face I've ever seen on a dog. Perse, as we fondly called him, and Tippy were the best of friends, male and female, about the same ages, old for dogs. When Tippy became ill, Perse followed her everywhere like a guardian angel protecting her and making sure that she made it home each night after roaming the woods or neighborhood. When she was safe, he could rest.

Every morning my dogs would greet me when I left for work and escort me down my driveway and miraculously would be waiting to escort me back up my driveway to my house every afternoon. I loved this daily attention from my dogs and felt particularly sad when Tippy couldn't make it up the road and back each day. It became a pointed search every morning for me to find her to check on her health before I went to work. Some short time after Tramp departed this earth, I found my Tippy, lying dead, in the cold, outside of my home.

I cannot explain all the emotions that flooded my heart and mind. I began to cry. And, at that very moment, I believed all dogs do go to heaven. God reminded me that dogs are his creation, for his pleasure and mine. Tippy had such a sweet presence that I realized she would be loved in heaven just as she was on earth. I immediately called Nancy to tell her the good and bad news! I could hear the smile in her voice as I agreed with her that our pets were not suffering anymore and in a better place. Two weeks later, my husband had to take Percy to have him put down from old age and grief. After Tippy left, he just could not rest here any longer.

Today, I have another dog, not a replacement because Tippy and Percy will never be forgotten or replaced. But, this time, I deeply love my dog and my dog loves me. I got him right after leaving my career of 27 years. I'm not sure I would have made it through bouts of stress and anxiety without him. His name is Hermie. He is a long-haired Dachshund. I think I have morphed into Nancy caring for my dog. Nancy and I have one more thing in common and Hermie enjoys all the luxuries of a pampered dog or should I say, a loved, with a capital L-O-V-E-D, dog!

AN ORDINARY BOY
By Rebecca Taksel

We make too much of the stars among us. I suppose it's inevitable: It's in the nature of stars that they dazzle us. Pancho wasn't a star. He was an ordinary boy, a tuxedo cat whose bow tie consisted of only a few white hairs under his chin. A black cat, then, with golden eyes. He had flashes of greatness, like his youthful high-jumping ability – table to top of high cabinet faster than the eye could follow. Otherwise he was just a nice cat, which is actually saying a very great deal.

Pancho walked up to my brother and me in the parking lot of a motel, came inside the room with us, ate whatever we gave him and otherwise sat quietly on the bed. We took him home and he made the journey, again, quietly. He was a small cat, not very vocal, not very demanding.

I lived with my mother, who was in her eighties when Pancho came to stay with us as the third member of our little household. She loved him as she had loved all the cats who'd lived with us before, but without fuss. At one point she did pronounce him "perfect." My mother and Pancho were companions for five years before she died at ninety. Pancho and I moved away from the place we'd lived with her.

Why are so many of our great lessons learned in the depths of grief? I grieved for my mother, walked through all the shifting sands of unbearable loss and happy memory and, finally, a deep sense of peace and gratitude: I had loved someone, and she had loved me. It seemed so simple, even trivial, when I tried to speak about it to others. But it was the greatest realization of my life. Through all the seasons of my grief, Pancho was with me, unprepossessing as he'd always been.

He died six years after my mother, and suddenly, unbearably, my grief was like something that had cracked open, a sky full of unexpected and terrifying lightning and noise and rain. I had always thought of Pancho as just himself, my nice, ordinary boy. In fact, I had never had much patience with people who spoke or wrote about animals as symbols or totems of human beings. Animals are, first and always, *themselves*. Where, then, did the unbearable thought come from that the last, the very last thread that connected me to my mother had been torn when Pancho died?

The thought grew and overwhelmed me. I raged against the whole dark universe. He was so small, demanded so little, took up so little space. Why had a vast, black emptiness reclaimed even that tiny life? What could it want with him? I went further, believed for a while that with Pancho had gone the last of what I recognized as my life, the last good thing in it.

Days went on, then a week, then a month, then another, until the day that I said to myself, *Pancho was perfection, the few drops of pure essence you were given in your life. The rest of your days are anointed by that perfection. Your mother saw it, and now you do, too.*

There are still days when life seems a cruel gift, promising that the longer you live the more you will be stripped of everything you love. But there are many more days, and not only the days when the whole world is beautiful and sunny and seems to demand a light and elevated mood, but also winter days, and rainy days, and dark windy days, when I know that loss deepens our hearts. In its embrace we finally know love.

AUTUMN WALK IN MIZZLING RAIN
By Nina Romano

At the lake when I walk my dog
Round the perimeter, he speaks softly
Of things long-ago forgotten.
He's older now and enjoys these serene
Moments of remembrance—just he and I again.
The kids grown and me over my empty-nest flutters.
No need to bark and bolt, jolting at the sound of birds
Careening in air, chirping, swooping, zooming for the fish.
He reminds me of his swagger days, dash and polished
Times, when he'd hidden my slipper for attention,
Or the time the police came at 2 AM
Because he'd cornered a baby opossum in the fichus.

We move slowly for this fall promenade,
Arthritis in his joints and my new knees
A trial getting used to. Leaves eddy and furl
And he scoots to where he thinks a mouse has scurried.
He lifts his head and tells me of the scents
He senses, tiny moles taking up their postings
For the tinge of cold soon to bring white flurries,
And the shoring, storing up of beaver in a stream,
A spring or slough back in the woods.

We round the outer edges of the lake where
Someone's prints have smudged in deep
Along with a trusty pilot dog that led him home.
It's time for us to go now, sport, what do you say?
He shakes his tail, thrusts his weight on two front paws,
His behind in a dare race me stance.
Not even if I could skip, my friend.

I sit on the wrought iron bench
With wooden back slats
And my patient pal, asks, So what now?
He plops down, resting his head on my feet,
Do you remember, he whispers, as wind
Blows my hair and his ears flop a bit,
I do not answer, but lean to stroke his once strong back,
As he whimpers a little
In quick profound old man's sleep,
Dreaming of our youth.

CARPE DIEM
By Michele Krause

May 15th, 2009
One hundred and sixty days have passed
Since I last touched your silken fur,
Thomas,
Since I squeezed you into me
And promised you that I was doing my best,
Placing you in the best hands I could,
And hoping we would share more days together.
But that was the last time I would hold you in my arms
And breathe in your sweet scented fur,
Though still I hold you now in my heart.
Oh, I miss you, Thomas!
You are still present in my world;
In each of my days;
You run across my thoughts
With your ears flopping behind you,
Joyously stretching your little legs
And opening your mouth in a smile.
I see you on your couch;
I look upon your favorite bed
And recall your many hours spent languorously

Drinking in the sounds of birdsong and Baroque music.
Tears paint my eyes salty
As I hear the songs we danced to
And recall your relaxed heaviness in my arms
As we'd swirl about the room
And then end on the sofa,
Your belly in the air
So I could rub you and gently drum to the rhythm.
I see you daily,
Not even in dreams,
But in waking life,
Painting you into the scenery in my mind's eye
That I may yet enjoy your company.
You bring me laughter
And still I weep for you and ache for you
And wish that I could have you back.
You delivered to me treasure
And I still reap the rewards
Of loving you.
In your very body you carried to me wisdom,
In your very body.
Whether or not wise yourself,
Your presence lent it to me
And I am filled with a soft sorrow for our parting.
Tomorrow another dog is coming here, Thomas.
Tomorrow I open my heart wide to receive a new love.
Tomorrow I will befriend another
Who comes to me because you cannot.
Your absence allows him a home.
Your absence grants him my heart
As a place to take his rest.
But you are not absent from my heart, Thomas.
You shall never be absent from my heart.
A new chapter begins tomorrow, Thomas,
And it is one in which you shall not appear,
Though you shall underwrite the script.
This dog who comes –
His name is Sparky –
Will feed on my love
And someday eat my heart
As you have,
But my love does not run low
And my heart renews its life
And you are ever-present to me

With each of its beats,
Though you are not present to me in form.
I will take this love with which you have endowed me
And I shall spend part of that treasure
To rescue a friend.
I shall invest this love in a new life
And feel in its growth
The roots and seed in you.
Tomorrow I shall step forward
Onto a new path from this
Change
That has separated us
And it may seem to onlookers that I am wandering
Away from you,
But I am not.
For loving you has given me the courage
To Dance a Timed Dance
With a new partner
Whose days may be as numbered as yours,
And, yes, I am afraid.
I confess it.
I am afraid.
You have taught me to be afraid
And you have also taught me that such fear
Simply does not matter.
Such fear is paltry
Compared to what is at stake
For both him *and* me.
And as I hear the first notes beginning
And prepare to step into Time,
I see your metronome tail wagging to me
Through memory
And I smile as I cry.

IN WITH THE NEW
By Kathleen Gerard

I don't believe in reincarnation, but I'm convinced my Yorkshire terrier must've lived a past life as a cat. For starters, Sissy loves fish - tuna, cod, and salmon are among her favorites. And she'll play for hours, chasing a tiny toy mouse on a string – if I'm willing to keep moving the bait. But the most notable feline quality about my dog is her tendency to hide. Sissy is primarily a housedog, but whenever I decide to take her for a walk, she disappears. I've seen her in action. Long before I even reach for her leash or put on my coat, she must read my mind and sense that our departure is imminent. She tucks her tail and skulks away like a clandestine C.I.A. operative. Her wet nose becomes the only thing visible when she squats even lower to the ground than she already is and crawls under the bed, the sofa; when she burrows beneath blankets; or her black-brown coat becomes camouflaged amid the shadows behind the toilet. At five pounds, it's easy for Sissy to vanish. And it's even easier for her to elude me, as whenever I spot her in full covert operation mode and try to sneak up and grab her, she quickly darts away, just shy of reach.

I've tried just about everything to break her of this habit. The word and even the letters W-A-L-K have been banned from my vernacular. (Yes, Sissy can even spell!) Furniture has been moved, blockaded. Treats dangled. And I hate to admit it, but I've even resorted to exiting the house and ringing the outside doorbell in the hope that the pretext of a potential visitor will coax her out of seclusion. All these lures might work once or twice, but Sissy catches on quickly. Any success I've had has been short-lived.

I believe there is probably an innate reason for Sissy's behavior - at least beyond my reincarnation theory. I've heard it said that when you make a conscious decision to get a dog, you don't get the dog you want, but rather, you get the dog you need. Such was the case of Sissy's entrance into my life.

It's a long story, but throughout the majority of my twenties, I lay wrapped in the cocoon of a ten-by-twelve foot bedroom in my mother's house. There had been surgery upon surgery to combat degenerating bones and soft tissue ruptures in my feet and ankles – and a slew of subsequent (and often unrelated) complications, including cancer. Some days it felt as though I were stuck in a cage, a prison. With one twist of my ankle, my life – and all my hopes and dreams – became deferred. In anger and frustration, I kicked and screamed and railed against my fate. What was supposed to be a "simple surgery" to get back on my feet, turned into thirteen surgeries and seventeen years of disability - and counting.

Somewhere along the way – I don't really know how or when it happened – that ten-by-twelve foot bedroom ultimately morphed into a very cozy sanctuary.

But that wasn't such a good thing.

Over the course of my disability, friends had gotten on with their lives - and rightfully so. There were advanced degrees, career booms, marriages (followed by divorces), families, houses and children. Other people's lives marched on - some without me. I felt alone, stuck, as though I were in a state of inertia. Yes, all the time off my feet had helped my writing career to flourish. But when a dear friend of mine said in passing, "When is all this surgery nonsense going to be over? When am I finally going to get the old Kathy back?" something rattled me to the core. The healthy life I had once taken for granted – and the one I had envisioned for myself – had vanished. The old Kathy was gone - and the sad fact was, she wasn't coming back. But who was the new Kathy?

I was now half-way through my thirties. I felt broken and damaged - inside and out. Riddled with insecurity because of the limitations imposed by my disability, I had shrunk away from people because I felt I could no longer meet their expectations.

"You're too isolated," my mother said one day. She was, no doubt, troubled by my restlessness. "What can you do to help yourself? What would bring you joy?"

Joy? The word instantly conjured my love for dogs - especially my fondness for Yorkshire terriers. I had grown up with one and another had kept me very good company in the early days of my disability. However, when Yorkie Number Two passed away, I felt I wasn't physically able to care for a new puppy. But by this point, I was semi-mobile. Maybe it was time? Maybe the unconditional love of a canine companion was exactly what I needed?

Thus my search began. I started perusing newspaper classified ads and the Internet. I contacted breeders and rescue centers. My homebound self suddenly felt inspired and motivated whenever I fastened my leg braces, reached for my crutches and dropped in at pet shops. I looked into at least a dozen dogs over the next six months, but because of one reason or another, I couldn't find a match - cost issues, dogs that had been sold before I got to them, health issues that made puppies unsalable, dogs too big or excitable for me to manage, or I simply "didn't fall in love," as they say.

My search was plagued by dead-ends, and I began to wonder if a new dog was really the answer. Although I had voiced those feelings, deep down I didn't believe them. Maybe the journey – the search in and of itself – was the real benefit? It had gotten me out of the house and back into the world on some level. Maybe the timing just wasn't right?

Eight months later and one hundred and thirty-seven miles from home, I finally found Sissy. Through a friend of a friend I discovered a breeder/broker who imported Yorkshire terriers from Brazil. When I contacted the breeder, she suggested I come for a visit and scope out her latest charges.

I tried not to be too hopeful, as it seemed a long shot, but my mother – a tireless, patient good sport – took on the three hour drive.

When we walked into the breeder's house, there had to be close to thirty Yorkies waiting to find homes. Yet none stole my heart enough to make a ten to fifteen-year commitment. I didn't feel it. Just as I was about to give up, my mother suggested we check the list of available pups one last time. When we cross-catalogued names and identification numbers, we realized there was one puppy we hadn't seen. When I inquired about her, the breeder hesitated, "Oh, I don't think you'd really want her - she has some issues, she's very shy . . ."

I looked to my mother, and she looked at me. She and I both knew I was an expert on shyness - among other neuroses. I shrugged and said, "What have we got to lose?"

The breeder scoured the pack. She went to the farthest corner of the dog pen, and peeling sleeping puppies one off another and checking ID tags, she finally uncovered a little runt. She was squashed and disheveled-looking, quivering and hiding at the bottom of the stack. She batted her eyes to the light a few times and looked around as if completely lost, but alas - she'd been found.

Sissy and I have been together three years. Among other lovable quirks, I guess you could say that cat-like hiding thing has been going on with her since the day we met. It's become sort of an exasperating game - a challenge, a battle of wills. But maybe it goes deeper than that. Maybe there's truth in the familiar adage that says, You don't get the dog you want, you get the one you need. I've come to believe that I need Sissy as much as she needs me. We are two of kind - two creatures who often have the tendency to hide from the world and people in it, but we've forged a bond. A necessary bond. Every time I'm successful in outsmarting and capturing her, and I slip on her leash and we step out together, I feel as though I can breathe again, as if I've been resurrected and liberated from all those years I spent in the tiny cocoon of my room. I don't know if it's her size or spunk or just the wag of her tail, but people and other dogs seem to naturally gravitate toward her. Once I can wrangle her from seclusion, Sissy is warm and friendly and trusting – and that's contagious. That five pound little ball of fur has drawn me out of my shell and taught me how to finally live again, with joy and acceptance, as the new me.

This piece was previously published (in a slightly different form) as "The New Me" in Good Dogs Doing Good (LaChance Publishing, 2010)

NEW DOG
By Nancy Brewka-Clark

What has four paws and a heart
As big as the full moon?
Now, it's a fuzz ball, all tumbles
and tangled legs, crazed by a
Shoelace.
Now it's a gangly goose of a pup,
Sliding on floorboards like a puck.

The love is unconditional,
Warm as flesh,
Strong as bone,
Saying with every breath,
"Home."

FLOWER POWER
By Cona Gregory-Adams

Our daughter, Lisa, had a habit of bringing him over for a "visit." Several times, she walked across the field to our house with the kitten in her arms and rang the bell. When either my husband, Bill, or I answered the door, she simply walked in and placed him on the floor without comment. I knew what she was doing . . . attempting to find a home for another stray. One of her "orphans" currently lived in our home and we had no desire for another.

But she knows us well; guessed correctly that we would fall in love with this tiny kitten, this totally unremarkable, grey-striped kitten. Someone had dumped him on Fountain City Road, at the bottom of the hill below our house. Lisa and her husband were driving home at night when their headlights revealed six baby kittens in the middle of the road.

"Scott, they'll be run over and killed," Lisa said.

Of course, they picked them up. Several lost cats have found a permanent home with them. Most are named for flowers, as are our two. They have Bonsai, Cricket, Pink and Vinca. They placed Sunflower and Marigold with our other daughter, Judy.

Naturally, Lisa's ploy worked. Sweet William came into our home four years ago and our lives haven't been the same since. His friendly, affectionate nature won the day and our resistance melted.

As soon as we agreed to keep him, Lisa said, "You'll have to think of the name of a flower for him."

It was a no-brainer for me to name the first cat they gave us, because it was a female. "That's easy," I said. "Petunias are my favorite flower. Her name is Petunia."

I couldn't think of the name of a flower for this little male kitten, but Scott named him Sweet William. I took a photo of him as a kitten, entered it in a pet-portrait contest, sponsored by our local newspaper. I wrote on back of the photo, "This is Sweet William, who lives up to his name."

His personality is anything but ordinary. When he gets wound up, he streaks through the house like a race car, bounding over and across whatever is in his path, be it couch or chair, dining room table, or human being. Our granddaughter, Chloe, calls him "Turbo Kitty." He is long past the kitten stage, but, since we took him to the vet for shots and neutering early on, he still behaves like a kitten. He fits T. S. Eliot's depiction of his cat in the poem, The Rum Tum Tugger, quite vividly.

Our other cat, Petunia, is beautiful with black ears and tail, thick white coat and a black and white patterned face. She was an adult when she came to live with us, as were all the other strays we've "adopted" over the years. Having a kitten in the house was a new experience for us.

Although Sweet William adopted me as his mother, Bill enjoys him almost as much as I do. When I'm doing laundry or working at the computer on a writing project, I hear Bill talking to him. When I'm away from the house, I return to a husband who laughingly describes his capers during my absence.

William is long and lean. We measured him at three feet, from the tip of his nose to the end of his tail. Petunia is short and fat, with small, dainty feet. Her surgery obviously produced a different effect from his. They now eat the same weight formula food for adult cats, but her short torso and her inactivity has caused her to be overweight.

When I came home after knee replacement surgery, Sweet William followed me into the bedroom, sniffed everything, then parked himself on my bed. He lay next to me day after day and never once stepped on my leg. Petunia didn't seem conscious of the bad leg but she's quite a talker. Every time you speak to her, she responds. They were a great comfort to me during my recovery.

Each one of Sweet William's siblings lives in a different home. Every cat in the litter possesses a unique personality. We hear reports of their antics from their owners and it gives us joy to know that they all thrive.

The person(s) who dumped those kittens have no idea of the blessings they've thrown away. When William climbs into my lap, curls himself into a ball, begins to purr and places his paws on my cheek, my heart melts like warm butter. It's more satisfying than a caramel sundae or a cheesecake brownie.

Pets offer both comedy and companionship. They give us older adults someone other than ourselves to talk with. They not only listen attentively, they talk back. I don't pretend to understand pet lingo, but I certainly have no trouble interpreting the language of love.

GOLDEN BOY
By Lea Gambina Pecora

Your tiny feet are paws of delicate perfection.
      Through half open eyes you drink in the world.
Your body trembles with gratitude – for me
                        for me.

You see who I am, don't you? Through those sleepy eyes.
You are not alarmed by my touch
      the opposite is true.
      I love that. I love you.

But I don't really know you.
You don't have a human soul!
      You can't know me…
      You can't love…
This is when you nuzzle in deeper
      with effortless intention you make me see
      your body melts with adoration – for me
                        for me.

On with my day
      one foot in front of the next.
I know what is waiting
      all the work at my desk.
All the people that need something and want it now.
      All the demands I place on myself
      the circles of upset I allow.

And then there is you
      my ultimate demand of the day
      completely dependent on me in every way.

>   Never doubting that I'll come through for you
>   the one constant in my life I know is true.

I'm starting to remember who I am
    as I eagerly greet your affection
    your squirms of excitement welcome me home.
You draw me into your fun, immersed in the moment of all you do.
    I love that. I love you.

After my third awakening in the middle of the night,
    twice for your needs and once for mine,
    I happily watch you sleep.
I marvel at your breathing – unaffected and pure.
    Are those smiles of enjoyment I see?
    Drinking in the world even in your dreams!
      I want that – for me
        for me.

Here I am in the dark before dawn, like so many times in the past,
    only now I have my golden boy to join me on my path.

You may not be my savior, in the body of this young pup,
    but the message you send me constantly
    one I clearly forgot and need reminding of
    is that I'm worthy, I'm beautiful,
      I am loved.

MAX
By Rosemary McKinley

    This small gray schnauzer-poodle mix came into our lives as my husband's dog. The man loves dogs and could not be without one. When our former canine was lost and never returned, Pete was on a quest for another companion. He researched the mix and sought out reputable places where we could buy one. I had much to say, mostly in disagreement to this longing. After all, I would be the one home more and the one who had to train and feed and clean up after a puppy. I did not want another pet.

    Our daughter conspired with Pete to persuade me and persuade me they did. I came close to drawing up a written contract spelling out who was going to feed and clean up after a puppy. We had a family meeting and both my husband and daughter agreed that they would be the ones to do the tasks required. Off the two of them went to buy the puppy. Of course, the first time the need for a clean up came, as often happens with a puppy, our daughter ran away. I strongly reminded her that she agreed to be part of the clean-up team. She reluctantly complied.

    As Max became a part of the household, it was quite apparent that he was Pete's dog and that Pete was the master. Max always had to have Pete in his vision or he would make a very unusual wailing sound, not a bark. He followed his master wherever he came and went at home. Max clung to him and even slept on his dog cushion right next to his master's side of the bed. Everyone who knew us noticed that Max seemed to think he was Pete's child! We laughed about it but it seemed to be true.

    A few years after Max became our pet, I was in a bad skiing accident; I sustained a nasty concussion in which I was confined to bed.

    I had to stay home for a week and rest. My head hurt so much that I couldn't do much else. Right next to my side of the bed lay Max, every minute of my recuperation. He stayed there, looking at me and resting, as well. I did not notice it at first, I was so miserable. Then I realized that the dog was not staying in the comfortable place that Max usually slept in. I couldn't even move his dog pillow, as I was not able to bend down. Regardless of his lack of comfort, Max stayed by my side day and night during that week. It was very comforting. He would look up at me as if to say that I would be all right.

As I dozed on and off that week, I would drop my arm down off the bed and Max would lick my fingers. Other times he would just look up at me as if to say that he was there for me. When the other family members came in and out of the house, Max remained by my side – not flinching in his watch.

As the week ended, Max's vigil waned and we both slowly went about our business as before. Max retreated to his favorite spot during the day, a couch in the downstairs den. Yet, even when I returned from work and took a nap, Max found his way back to his watch. He wanted to be sure that I was recovering and returning to normal. Canines do not need words to express their concern even for people who did not originally want them.

Near the end of Max's life, it was I who cared for him. He was sick and could hardly walk up and down the stairs. I carried him when he needed it and cleaned up after him because I knew he couldn't help himself. I never forgot the comfort he gave me when I was in pain. It was I who held him in the vet's office when he said his last goodbye.

HOW A BROWN BABY BUNNY CHANGED EVERYTHING
By Sarah Goodwin-Nguyen

A little brown bunny changed the path of one human life – mine. But on the day we took him home, my fiance, Andy, and I just thought he was really cute. We had a mimosa buzz after a holiday brunch, and walked into a pet store on New York City's Lower East Side "just to look."

Mama bunny and her litter were all adorable, of course, with their pointy ears and gangly back legs all jostling for room in the too small glass tank. There were black ones, white ones, and one single brown bunny. The pet store owner, spotting a sucker, decided I must hold one. I pointed to the brown one, and the pet store owner put him in my arms. Andy and I knew nothing about rabbits, but followed all the shopkeeper's advice by purchasing what we later learned was the wrong cage and the wrong food. Andy also chose a white litter-mate, another male, for his companion.

I still remember that first night, how we stared at the little rabbits, staring back at us from their cage. They'd munch a strand of hay, not taking their eyes off us, ears up. I thought they looked expectant, but not afraid. We named the brown bunny Pumpkin and the white one Lemon. We let them out of their cage and enjoyed the novelty of watching rabbits exploring our Manhattan studio apartment.

Back then, my life was very different. I was using my writing degree to work for a literary agency. My job was acquiring foreign distribution rights to offer to agents and publishers in foreign countries. I wrote creatively on the side, short stories and poetry mostly. I only had a vague concern about animals and the environment

I was also, in many ways, profoundly unhappy. New York City, which years ago had seemed so exciting and promising, felt like wasteland as I matured: not enough green, not enough room, dirty air, and polluted rivers. I took antidepressants to cope with a life that often seemed empty.

My love for those first two rabbits was like a gateway to an appreciation of animals and nature. In New York, I began volunteering with Rabbit Rescue and Rehab and in the "exotics" room of the Harlem SPCA. Seeing those rabbits, rodents, ferrets, and birds living in crowded city shelters, I started longing for a very different landscape for them – and for myself.

Soon after our wedding, my husband and I packed up the rabbits – which by then numbered three. We moved from the Big Apple to the Florida Keys. My experience volunteering with "exotics" landed me my first job with wildlife: cleaning cages at the Wildlife Rescue of the Florida Keys. A job I never would have applied for if that shopkeeper not put a little brown bunny in my arms.

Jump forward ten years, and be astounded by the fact that I kicked the Prozac through helping animals. At the aquarium, there was Hector, the hawksbill sea turtle, who loved his shell scratched and shook with glee like a golden retriever if you used a pool brush. At the wild bird rehabilitation center, there was Hermes, the peregrine falcon, who I rescued from a mangrove tree where he waited to die after breaking his wing and falling to the sea. There is Bonnie, the broadwing hawk, who still flies to my arm every day for her dinner.

Some days, I miss Mayhem, the homeless prairie dog, for whom I finally found a home and a mate. I think about the oddball critters I have made deep connections with through the years – a ground squirrel, a tortoise, a grouper, and an octopus – and I smile.

I have been privileged to hand-feed nurse sharks in front of awestruck crowds. Once, I jumped into shallow water to hold up a wild bottlenose dolphin who was trying to beach himself. He and I spent hours, skin on skin, eye to eye before the trucks came with the equipment to try to keep him alive. While working for the butterfly conservatory, I held butterfly pupae in my hand, felt them twitch, saw them open, watched the emergence of the butterfly who hangs its wings to dry for hours, patient, though it has but days left to live.

Of course, there have been other rabbits – lots of rabbits: Wilbur, Bolter, Iggy, Bean, and Sweetpea. There were shelter rabbits, rescue rabbits and feral rabbits. I was once involved in a failed rabbit rescue group in the Lower Keys. After getting to know rabbits, I became more politically active, more of an advocate for animals, conservation of wildlife and the environment.

Now, our original two rabbits, Pumpkin and Lemon, are nearly eleven years old and in their golden years. We have four rabbits altogether, and a rat and a cat as well. My little brown bunny is arthritic and has kidney troubles. I am not sure how much longer we have. I repay him for changing my life as best as I can, taking him out in the yard to enjoy the sunshine and fresh grass, giving him good things to eat, petting him maybe a little more than the other animals. I put the heater next to his cage when it's cold and I say nothing when he pees under the bed. How else can I thank him?

My writing changed too, more nonfiction began to emerge. I suddenly wanted to share my knowledge of the creatures with which we share the Earth – it really is amazing, the diversity on this planet. If only we appreciated it more and took better care of it.

I opened myself up to love a little brown rabbit, and the rest of the planet came tumbling in.

WHO?
By Rosalie Ferrer Kramer

Who lives in our house that looks so sad,
Who has a tail that says, "I'm glad?

Who has brown eyes and a nose so cold?
Who acts like a baby although he's old?

Who is the critter my children adore,
Who puts muddy paws on my clean floor?

Who makes my sons laugh when kissing them happy,
Who leaps on their wheel chairs and licks them sappy?

Who makes them giggle with his silly tricks,
Who helps them feel better when they were sick?

Who can solve the puzzle of this "Who" game?
Why our dog Spooky can 'cus that's his name.

IN MY DOG'S EYES
By Paul S. Piper

In my dog's eyes sit Buddhist
monks, silent and illuminated.

There are hints of cinnamon
and chocolate. There is a sunny day

and a street where children skip
and play. There is a meadow that carries

to the sky, and a sky that gives
me wings, then buries my feet

in the mud. In my dog's eyes
is a whisper and a laugh; the nudge

of a joke. Always smiling, they never
judge; before his eyes

I can only fail myself. In my dog's
eyes is a place where words

surrender to stars. A gaze
that instantly forgives and heals.

A light from that strange land
has entered me, impossible to extinguish,

its blessing kindled forever.

PEPPER: THE PROSAIC PIGEON
By John R. Chega

I have lived a solitary lifestyle for many years, but it wasn't until an event took place recently that I realised how isolated and empty my life was.

My home is in a downtown high-rise apartment building in Calgary, Alberta. One day in January I was watching a winter storm from my fifth floor living room window when I witnessed, what I thought, was a curious event.

The weather had created a veil of blowing snow and I could hardly see the neighboring buildings that were usually visible from my window. The temperature was a brutal -25 Celsius/-13 Fahrenheit and the wind was bending the trees and making outdoor travel a dangerous experience.

As I was watching, a lady fighting against the wind trudged through the snow in the parking lot next to my building. At one point, she hesitated in her walk and gave a nudge with her boot to a black spot on the snow in front of her. To her astonishment and mine too, the black spot moved! She took a step backwards, looked a little more intently at it and then proceeded on her way. After a few steps she hesitated once more, turning to look back at the black spot and I could almost see her indecision, but after a moment she shrugged her shoulders and continued on her way.

Not knowing why, or what I'd expected to find, I decided to venture out and see what the black spot was. I put on a sweater, my heavy canvas parka, insulated winter boots, toque, scarf and woollen mitts and headed outdoors. In all honesty, I really don't know why I did that. I usually mind my own business and leave the rest of the world to its own devices but something inside told me to go and see what was going on.

When I got to the place where I saw the lady stop, I found a small pigeon sitting in a frozen car wheel rut half covered by snow. I knew if I left it there it would die so I reached down, folded its wings together and tucked the pigeon into my coat against my chest.

There is a strict "no pets" policy in my building and the rule says we are not even allowed to bring pets in the door, but I thought it was more important to save a life than follow a rule, so I surreptitiously proceeded to my apartment.

Once we got to my apartment I removed my winter gear and went over to have a closer look at him. What I discovered surprised me. One of the pigeon's feet was totally encased in ice and there was a strip of beet red flesh running down the length of his back between his wings from his neckline to his tail.

It looked like he'd been plucked clean, and right at the base of this wound was another chunk of ice about the size of a small ice cube. I didn't want to hurt him but I had to remove the ice before it froze him even though he was indoors. I knew he was in pain but I didn't know what I could do for him. I've had the experience of freezing my fingers and toes and I knew the intense ache that happens when frozen flesh begins to thaw.

Once I'd taken the ice off the little fellow I stroked the back of his neck and softly crooned to him so he could relax and go to sleep. It worked! He perched himself on one foot, tucked his beak into his chest and went to sleep. He didn't move for nearly 2 days.

I knew I should leave him alone but every once in a while I would go over to see if he was still alive. I'd gently stroke him while talking in a soft voice, he would open his eyes and look at me and I would croon to him in as calming and soothing voice tone as I could muster. I would tell him he was alright now, he was safe, and to just go to sleep and everything would be alright.

While he was sleeping I arranged a bowl of water and went out to the store to buy some multigrain bread that he could eat when he woke up. Originally I'd given him the name "Peter" because I thought "Peter Pigeon" had a nice ring to it. But about three hours after he woke up, on the second day, and began eating, I renamed him "Pepper;" it was either "Pepper" or "Pig" because when he found that bread he went to town. I mean he didn't even give my presence any attention at all, he was busy eating and he had no intention of being distracted. He was hungry and I was encouraged to see that he had an appetite.

For the next day or so, Pepper would wake up for ten or fifteen minutes, eat something and then go back to sleep. The noise from my television, my movements back and forth to the kitchen and sometimes passing close by his perch didn't seem to bother him. And at least once every hour I'd sit down in front of him and gently stroke the back of his neck and talk to him. I'd tell him in a soft voice that he was "a good boy and that everything would be okay." I did this as often as possible so he would feel safe and not be afraid. I wanted him to relax and get better.

I fed Pepper a combination of foods I thought would promote quicker healing. I bought soft calcium-enriched energy bars, multigrain bread and fresh water with a touch of milk to enhance the calcium content. Feathers, like bones, consist mainly of calcium and I was trying to give Pepper the best possible chance of a full recovery.

I have to admit that having another life form in such close proximity was, at times, inconvenient. It wasn't customary for me to have to consider the noise level coming from the TV or how I usually slammed the doors of my cupboards and drawers. I even refrained from vacuuming because I thought the noise would startle him and he would freak out and hurt himself. But on the other hand, I realised I enjoyed having him there.

It was pleasant every once in a while to look over and see him peacefully sleeping on the back of the couch or watching him preen his feathers and stretch his wings. In observing his actions I was amazed to learn how smart he was. I learned that birds, at least the common pigeon, don't just peck at their food. Pepper would take a piece of the bread in his beak and then twist his head quickly, flick his head sideways, and in doing so would tear a small piece of bread from the larger slice. In this way he would also flick little portions of bread all over the room and I soon had to place a full sized bed sheet under the towel and over the whole couch to keep his eating habits contained in one place.

He also showed me how intelligent he was. If I gave him a piece of bread that was too large to eat in one sitting, the piece left behind would get hard. I was surprised to see Pepper pick up the hard piece of bread and drop it in his water bowl. After a few minutes the water softened the hard bread and Pepper would reach inside the bowl and take a piece of soft bread to eat. The little bugger had found a way to soften the hard bread to make his dining a more palatable experience! He was also eating the bread and getting a drink of water at the same time. Smart boy!

On the morning of the 8th day Pepper died. When I came into the room that morning he was standing on both legs but was leaning against the wall. I took a bread pan and lined it with a wool toque and placed him in this "nest like" apparatus. He looked at me silently with his big golden rimmed brown eyes and was more docile than I'd ever seen him. I was stroking the back of his neck gently and telling him what a good boy he was when his nose started to bleed, he lowered his head, and he died. I experienced an almost overwhelming sense of loss.

After a while I said a prayer, wrapped his body in the wool toque and recycled him. I knew in my heart Pepper's Spirit had left, and the body that held that innocent Spirit was natural compost for Mother Earth, so I let HER have it.

Having Pepper in my life was a great experience. It made me realise that without someone, or something to care for and take care of, the human experience is a less fulfilling experience.

Since then I have involved myself in more "people oriented" activities and actually started to make some friends. I think of Pepper often and even recognize what must be members of his family when I see pigeons with his colouring.

I miss Pepper, and in his honor, I've decided that from this time forward I will regard "ALL" life forms as gifts from God and respect as many of them as possible in my own limited time on this earth.

DEVOTED EYES
By Louise Webster

I return home broken and troubled.
The loss of my legs so great,
"Who am I now?" I wonder.
What shall be my fate?

My family is protective.
They satisfy every whim.
Yet I am so lonely,
Can't let people in.

Then comes that familiar jangle
Of an exuberant loyal friend.
But will I disappoint my dog?
Disabled as I am.

He jumps on the bed to lick me.
Their hands gently shoo him away.
Worried I might be hurt
But, "No, No," let him stay.

Tentatively he sniffs me,
Those strange and foreign smells.
Of fever, pain and death too close.
He knows I've not been well.

I feel his muzzle nudge me.
Soon kisses melt my heart.
I pet his fur and scratch his neck,
Each healing has its start.

Throughout my recovery,
He has been by my side.
Silently encouraging me,
With his ever devoted eyes.

THE LANGUAGE OF LOVE
By Judy Kirk

When you live alone,
it's easy for minutes to drag into hours,
quiet times to darken with loneliness.
Then along comes some
furry or feathery,
hairy or lizardy
creature and suddenly,
the emptiness in a room fills up.

Pets know the language of love
as surely as humans.
Each meow of my cat
is a hearty Hello,
each soft yip whispers, You're not alone,
and the pawing at my face
or a nuzzle at my hand
is a simple caress
that says, I love you.

THE GRAY GHOST
By Elaine Morgan

I often shook my head during the relationship I had with a crippled Mockingbird and wondered if he had warned the neighbor's tom cat, an old Tabby Infantryman, with a vigorous rapidly repeated battle song or two before he flew that final mission. It was early spring, and I figured the Mockingbird was probably defending a nest full of potential hatchlings in a low-growing hedge or bush. On the other hand, he might simply have been playing "cat roulette" and exhibiting the usual territorial, aggressive nature common to that species. After we were better acquainted, I figured it was the latter of the two.

The Mockingbird was brought to me in a cardboard shoe box. I was a licensed wildlife rehabilitator for many years, but I cringed when I opened the box to take a look.

He had a curled-up left foot, no tail feathers, cat fang and claw puncture wounds, and the permanent injuries which would forever alter his natural existence... a left shoulder fracture, one-half of the left wing was missing, and one-quarter of the right wing had also been "amputated" by the old tom cat. It was obvious that this bird had put up one heck of a fight, but I was saddened by the outcome of the battle. What I expected to see was pain and fear in the Mockingbird's eyes, but what I saw instead was a curious combination of determination and defiance. I felt my eyebrows knit together as I wondered if it could be possible. Then I peered into those seemingly determined, defiant steel gray eyes and somberly whispered, "Your dive-bombing days are over, little soldier."

Euthanasia was the most compassionate solution, but it was late on a Saturday and I had no choice but to hold the bird over until Monday morning. I knew the healing skills I had to offer as a licensed wildlife rehabilitator were inadequate for the situation.

The best I could do was to make the bird as comfortable as possible. Medical attention consisted of food, water, a "shoe splint" for the broken foot, an antibiotic to fight infection and, most importantly, rest and quiet from the trauma in a covered cage in a back room of the house.

I did not expect the bird to last through the night. However, the following morning I was stunned to find myself looking into those steely gray eyes again, eyes full of life and a curious intent to survive in spite of the hand the fates had dealt it. Knowing the odds were against it, I again questioned the validity of what I thought I saw in those eyes.

On Monday morning, the Mockingbird was alert, upright, eating on his own, and challenging me with his indomitable spirit. Reluctantly, I followed the dictates of my heart instead of my head, and gave the bird the benefit of a very doubtful situation. I wondered if the bird realized he would never fly again and, even if he did manage to survive, didn't he know he would gain his life and lose his freedom? I also wondered of what possible use a wild, crippled Mockingbird would be to me, even as an educational animal.

Summer arrived that year like a painter with a bucketful of green enamel, splashing everything in sight. It was a time of renewed life and healing, and somehow the Mockingbird insinuated himself into the magic of the season. He was strong again, able to perch on one foot, and I knew it was time to incorporate him into the aviary room with the other handicapped wild bird residents of the household. The Mockingbird now had his own large flight cage in front of a set of double windows overlooking the back property, and the companionship of two parakeets, a handicapped English Sparrow and a blind Grackle who was in my care ever since he was a nestling.

I named the Mockingbird Mosby, The Gray Ghost, after that notoriously wily Confederate Civil War General who slipped in and out of enemy lines and camps with the skill of a disembodied spirit. Knowing the bird would never slip in and out of anything again, I wondered if he would adjust to his new life on the inside lines.

Mosby had four new companions who were tame and noisy. The aviary room was full of life with a raucous din continually emanating from within it. There would also be the temporary company of all those orphaned nestlings and fledglings I raised seasonally in that room until they were mature enough to go wild again in the outdoor aviary prior to release back into the wild. I thought Mosby would respond, but he was silent the rest of that year, perched on a tree branch, quietly starting out of the double windows. I felt uneasy and wondered if I had misread his eyes on the day we met.

One day in late February of the following year, I was surprised to hear the shrieking of a Blue Jay inside of the house. I wondered how it had gotten in, and I figured it had slipped inside undetected when I had opened the back door to let the family dogs out. I quickly grabbed the bird net and went searching through the room to find that noisy Jay.

I became even more puzzled when I also heard the loud calling of a Phoebe, followed by the song of a White-Throated Sparrow and a Baltimore Oriole, all of the calls and songs loud and in a half-dozen rapidly repeated succession. I followed the pitch of where the calls seemed to be originating from.

My search led me to the doorway of the aviary room and I stood there wide-eyed and transfixed, listening and watching the movement of Mosby's throat and open beak.

I felt my face screw up and tears well in my eyes. I saw the blind Grackle lower his head to one side and cock an ear in Mosby's direction, while the noisy parakeets fell silent. The room was still except for what I imagined to be the song of a Nightingale as Mosby slipped into melodious calls even I could not identify. His repertoire was awesome and, in that instant, I recognized him to be an old, well-seasoned warrior.

It was mating season again, and all of the migratory birds had arrived back into the area to nest, their arrival apparently triggering within Mosby an old reason for living in a new way. He had another mission to fly. This time without wings and he was determined, I could tell, to continue to chase rivals and defend his new territory; even if it had to be from a set of double windows. He had chosen to adapt and to adjust and he was directed by the strongest movement of will that I had ever witnessed.

Spring and summer brought the usual groups of children to the house to be educated about the value of wildlife. My routine was altered because of Mosby. On the tour of the aviary room, I had to add to my presentation: "Girls and boys, that is not a Blue Jay which you think you are hearing. It's a Mockingbird. His legal name is Mimus Polyglottos-Polyglottos, and he is in the family of Mimidae. I call him Mosby, The Gray Ghost, for obvious reasons and for one which is not so obvious. Mosby got into a fight with an old tom cat and he lived to sing about it. He's wild, territorial, and he prefers that you observe him from a distance."

Two years later, I found myself in a fight for my own life. I arrived home one day with a diagnosis of cancer. I knew the odds were against me, just as they had been against Mosby at one time. With a heavily burdened heart and spirit, I walked into the aviary room and pulled a chair up in front of Mosby's flight cage. I sat down, listened to his loud miming, and I stared into those steely, determined pale gray eyes. After a few moments of quiet reflection, I loudly proclaimed in chorus in a roomful of raucous din, "If you could do it Mosby, I can do it, too! I'll live to sing about it and fly in spirit just as you have!" And, that's exactly what I did.

DREAM GIRL
By Elynne Chaplik-Aleskow

My sisters and I stood at the living room window and watched my father get out of the car holding a brown cardboard box. In anticipation my sister Susan, who was two years old, took one look at the box and promptly threw up. So began her childhood fear of dogs.

To me this was my personal new puppy even though I had to share her with my family. My dad entered the apartment holding the box. He lowered it so I could see what was inside and that was the first moment I saw our new German Shepherd, Dream Girl.

It was a hot summer afternoon. My cousins Eddie and Larry were visiting. Being the tomboy that I was, that was always a special treat. My sister Linda always complained that during our games of cowboy and Indians she was the first to get killed off.

I picked up the new puppy and we all headed to our backyard to play Rin Tin Tin. We were utterly amazed at how quickly Dream Girl became one of us. Every time we shot Linda and she fell to the ground, our genius puppy would go to her and put her paw on the body.

We were playing for an hour or so when Dream Girl collapsed. We all ran to her standing over her in a circle. She did not move. I ran into the apartment yelling for my father to come. "The puppy is dead," I screamed. He ran out to the yard and informed us that playing in the hot sun, the puppy had fainted. She needed shade and water. "Remember," he cautioned, "she is just a baby herself."

As I recall this memory, I have a knot in my stomach and a longing for the dog who was to become my closest friend and whom I loved with all my heart.

My family moved to a house within the next year. Most unfortunately, my mother was not a dog lover. With our new white carpet, Dream Girl was only allowed in certain rooms of the house. I objected with all the arguments I could think of but I lost.

One night there was a terrible rainstorm. The lightening was blinding and the thunder was deafening. As I walked down the stairs toward the garage, I saw water seeping in under the door. My first thought was of Dream Girl. She had been out in the garage. As I opened the door my mother was yelling, "Do not open that door." The flooded garage water knocked me over as it entered the house. Swimming on top of it all was my precious dog. She swam to me and started licking me as I sat soaked on the floor. I held her tight and kissed her back.

My mother was so distracted by the flood that she did not even notice that my German Shepherd and I headed upstairs to my bedroom. I took a towel and tenderly dried her. That night she slept with me in my bedroom, white carpet and all.

My dad had a German Shepherd when he was a boy. He loved them. His dog appeared on his doorstep one night during a storm so he called him Stormy. This dog became my father's personal protector. One day one of my dad's buddies came up behind him and playfully put a chokehold on him. Stormy plunged toward the boy and if my dad had not caught the leash, the dog would have attacked. My dad was always convinced that Stormy was a lost military dog. One day as he came so he left.

When my father bought Dream Girl, her papers stated she was the great, great granddaughter of Rin Tin Tin the Third. I was very proud of this pedigree. Even so my dad claimed she was not as smart as his dog because he had trouble housebreaking her. I, on the other hand, thought she was not only smart but also as loving and attentive as one could hope for in any friend. She understood me like no human could.

One day my mother called for a family meeting. I was caught completely off guard as to her agenda. My mother, the non-lover of dogs, informed us that before her new baby, my third sister, was born, the dog must go. She was afraid to have a dog in the family with an infant. I knew, of course, that she had finally found an excuse to get rid of the dog she never really wanted.

I objected to the point that I demanded a family vote, sure that the rest of us would vote down my mother. To my absolute shock I was the only one who voted for Dream Girl to stay. I was devastated. I just stared at the hands raised. I was sure that my sisters were afraid to vote against my mother. But my father? How had she gotten to him too?

I ran from the meeting crying and locked myself in the bathroom. My parents tried to bribe away my pain with offers of a new bicycle or perhaps a radio. I was true to my Dream Girl. I stopped speaking to all of them.

When my father sold my dog, I begged the couple who bought her to let me call them to ask about her. They told me that there was a girl similar to my height and weight who would wait for the school bus at the corner and that whenever Dream Girl saw her she would whine and cry.

       To this day my heart longs for my first dog and the friendship she gave to me. Whenever I see a German Shepherd, I stop and lovingly stroke the memory of my Dream Girl.

ANGEL BOY
By Jean Varda

purring rubbing bumping
miniature cougar head
happy with ground chicken liver
watching birds from windows
all night comforting my bed

CARING FOR TEDDY
By Diana M. Amadeo

The one absolutely unselfish friend that man can have in this selfish world, the one that never deserts him, the one that never proves ungrateful or treacherous, is his dog... He will kiss the hand that has no food to offer; he will lick the wounds and sores that come in encounter with the roughness of the world... When all other friends desert, he remains. ~ George G. Vest

When our third child was about a year old, the pressure was on to get a dog. During spring break I took the kids to the Humane Society. None of the pets there tugged at our heartstrings. We were halfway out the door when an elderly man arrived with a tiny dog that was so dirty it was impossible to determine his color. The man relayed that the dog had just been retrieved from the arms of his sister – a hospice patient that had chosen to die in her home. He guessed that the poodle was about a year old.

We asked to see the dog and found him infested with fleas. When left alone with the kids, he ran around them, over them and on them. He'd jump up and plant big wet kisses on their lips. Then tiring of the kids, he suddenly propelled himself up onto my chair, licked my cheek, put his head on my shoulder and fell asleep.

"What is his name?" I whispered to the old man.

"Teddy," the old man said quietly. "She called him that, but you can change it."

It was an impulse decision. The kids and I debated for just a few minutes. I signed papers to adopt the dirty poodle with a promise to have him seen ASAP by a veterinarian.

There was never a question that we would keep his name. When we got Teddy home, I immediately flea dipped him. He turned out to be snow white. Teddy liked getting his teeth brushed and his hair combed. Then my husband came home from work. Oops. I forgot to let him know of our new arrival.

And so began our 15 year odyssey.

Teddy wasn't housebroken. He wasn't even tame. He wasn't a perfect dog. But his imperfection became downright endearing.

Teddy did not like being alone. There wasn't a cage that could hold him, a door he couldn't open and a lock that he couldn't figure out. On his first time alone in our home, he jumped up on my son's desk and pulled off the screen to the window. He proceeded to tear the screen to shreds.

His first Christmas with us involved unwrapping gifts under the tree, eating the concealed chocolate and wiping his face all over my beige carpet. When we got home, he proudly brought us in to show his handiwork. I was horrified and then relieved to find that it was only chocolate and not what I had feared on the rug. How could such a little dog make such a profound mess?

When we had an oak staircase put in the home, Teddy somehow found his way around the barricades and left perfect doggy prints on the newly polyurethaned stairs. Our French Canadian carpenter knew no English, but the next day cried out in exasperation, "Teddy, no, no, no!"

About the same time we adopted Teddy, we also acquired a kitty; the runt of the litter. As an adult, she and Teddy were the same size. This cat had no fear. If Teddy should happen to walk by as she was dozing in the chair, out would come a paw and swat him in the face. The poor dog would just look around confused. If he dared ignore her, she would meow angrily, propel herself forward and begin to chase him. Within seconds there would be a total reversal and Teddy would be chasing her.

On one of these merry chases he succeeded in toppling the Christmas tree – and shattering some pretty expensive heirloom ornaments.

As our family grew, we added a second story four-season porch to our home. The contractor worked steadily for awhile and then left it unfinished while waiting for the windows to arrive. One morning Teddy made his way onto the porch, spied the open cut-outs and took off at full speed. Like the old Mighty Dog commercial, he soared through the air before landing on the ground 2 floors below. Immediately, he began to cry, holding up his paw then limp. The cat sprang to the window ledge and began to meow in mockery. Teddy looked up to the cat and took off towards the house, suddenly cured.

Teddy loved the great outdoors. We went bye-bye on errands and took long daily walks. Being so low to the ground, he got dirty easily from the road's gravel and slush. When we got back home, he'd race to the kitchen sink and wait for me to hoist him up for his daily bath. His favorite part of the ritual was being wrapped in a big warm towel and being cuddled like a baby.

After a severe exacerbation of multiple sclerosis, I was left relatively immobile with visual impairment and hearing loss. Teddy never left my side. He'd lick away my tears of self pity and place his paw compassionately over my weak hands. Wheelchairs and crutches followed, with Teddy by my side, smiling and wagging his tail joyously at my physical progress. Spasticity can be very painful. Teddy always seemed to know when I was in pain. He would jump up on my lap, lay his head upon my chest and give me comfort. His activity level slowed during my ten year rehabilitation. We were inseparable. He was my shadow.

As Teddy aged, he could no longer open doors or pick locks. If my bedroom door was shut, he would lay down outside, waiting for me to awaken. My older children went off to college and graduated. My youngest, who was a baby when we adopted Teddy, was beginning high school. He knew her routine. Everyday she'd call between 3 and 5 to be picked up from her various after school activities. As soon as the phone would ring, he'd run to the door and wait for his sweater to be applied so we could go bye-bye.

After we had Teddy for a decade and a half, his eyes began to dim with cataracts and his hearing progressively worsened. He would have occasional bouts of arthritic pain and developed lateral sclerosis of the spine. When he couldn't make it up the stairs, we'd carried him. Despite cleaning and brushing, his teeth began to fall out and he was prone to foul gum disease. He started acting confused and frightened easily. Two years before, when he first showed signs of heart disease, I had talked euthanasia with the vet. Then Teddy would rebound miraculously and life went on. But now, despite meds of all sorts, it looked like his entire body was simply shutting down. It was time to ease his suffering.

Teddy seemed to sense the pain of our decision and tried to tell us that it was okay. When my daughter and I brought Teddy to the vet for the final time, we took turns holding him and crying. Teddy laid his head on our chests and nuzzled. We stayed with him until he breathed his last. We decided to leave him with his sweater on for the cremation so the handlers would know to handle him with the care and respect he deserved.

I believe that the spirit of a living being never dies. For a week following his death, the soft clinking of his dog tags, brought me comfort.

And then I had a dream: across from me, on a stuffed lounger, sat Teddy. He was so human-like with his legs crossed. In one paw he held a cigar. In the other hand was a double bourbon. He smiled and said, "I was dying anyway, don't sweat it." Then he tipped his glass in salute and was gone.

Those who know me would say that the dream was totally out of character. If I was visualizing Teddy it would be in clouds with wings. But in recalling his antics, the dream *was* Teddy. He wasn't perfect. He was silly. He didn't come off as too smart. Teddy lived his life to the fullest, his way. And now his time has come. There are no regrets.

Previously published in Dogs and the Women Who Love Them
(Angel Animals Network)

REST, MY SWEET GIRL
By Linda O'Connell

When you were a pup
you frolicked in open fields and
feathers from our bed pillows.
You teethed on my shoes and gnawed
legs of every wooden table.

The kids dressed you up and hugged your neck.
I held you snuggle-close when I was sad.
Your wavy fur sopped my tears,
your little body curled into mine
gave me something to hold when everyone let go.

Before the children, you were my Spaniel-Waniel baby,
every FIRST was ours.
You ran with the wind but always returned to my side.
We spoke the same language. I'm sorry for that time I barked.
I could see the understanding in your sweet expression.

Now, as you snooze through old age,
may you be blessed with a field of dreams to romp in,
the wind always blowing against your face,
and the thrill of finally catching that elusive squirrel.
Lay down your weary head. Rest. Sleep peacefully, old girl.

SPUNKY
By Cherise Wyneken

Dad stood in front of the bathroom sink – hanging on for dear life as he tried to shave. Spring was in the air as the winter of his life began. Mama had enjoyed an extra year with him because of the radiation treatment for esophageal cancer, but she knew it wouldn't last. On his last visit to Florida, I had watched him coming slowly up the walkway from the plane and knew he was near the end.

When the time came, Mama would need my help with burial arrangements, death certificates, and the like. I kept juggling the days – so I wouldn't be away from my own home too long. Three of our four children lived in the San Francisco Bay Area and were faithful in going out to Walnut Creek, to help my mother and to visit Dad. But I was far away and worried. One day on the phone, Mama told me that our son's girlfriend, had come out to see them on the Greyhound Bus. Under her hippie serape she had hidden a tiny puppy in the palm of her hand. A gift for my parents.

"Great," I stormed. "That's all Mama needs now. A puppy to train and care for."

Mama fell in love with him at once. She prepared a penned-in nook in the corner of the kitchen for him to sleep. Somehow he always managed to escape and go looking for her, so they named him Spunky. Of an uncertain breed, he appeared to be part Corgi with a short chestnut colored hide and ears that stood straight up. Mama began to wonder whether they should keep him as her attention to Spunky seemed to be making Dad jealous.

When Dad died, Spunky proved to be a godsend for Mama. I stayed for awhile to help her settle her affairs. Then everyone was gone. As she curled up on the sofa – in a funk of mourning – Spunky's urgent calls to go outside forced her to get up and let him out. He needed to be trained and fed. He was a puppy after all. She began to buy him toys and played tug of war with him. He'd whine to be let up on her lap as she listened to the evening news. When she went out with family or friends she didn't have to go home to an empty house. Spunky always jumped for joy in his welcome-home routine. Mama now had someone to talk to in the lonely hours. Spunky outgrew his corner in the kitchen and ended up sleeping on Mama's bed. He growled and barked at every suspicious sound, even at the squirrels as he chased them up the tall pine tree in the back. And she always knew what day it was when the garbage men arrived. It was Spunky's day to bark without restraint.

Through yips and yaps, he carried on a love affair with a dog across the street. They were both confined to their yards, but one day, Dolly got out and into Mama's yard. The dogs stood staring at each other, not knowing what to do with their flaring emotions. "Poor old Spunky," Mama chuckled. "You've been a monk too long."

In time Mama began to need help herself. A series of housekeepers were stop-gaps to her going into a personal care home. My brother invited her to come live with them in Southern California. Spunky didn't like it so Mama brought him home. Eventually we found a live-in woman. Then Spunky began leaving "offerings" on the living room rug and the woman stomped out. We encouraged Mama to move to one of the fancy new retirement places. But no. Not if Spunky couldn't come along. As he aged, Spunky began having more and more accidents in the house that Mama couldn't deal with.

"I think it's time you had Spunky put to sleep," I said one day. "He's too old for you to handle. It won't be so bad for him," I added. "You can hold him on your lap and he won't feel anything."

Reluctantly – she consented. Our daughter brought her grandmother a stuffed toy dog, and even though she doesn't like pet animals, she kissed Spunky good-bye. But Spunky still had his spunk and put on such a hale and hearty act in front of the vet that Mama took him home again. She renamed him Lazarus. Things went on the same for a while until one night Mama heard the dog convulsing. She called her friend Minette in the morning and asked her to take them to the vet's for a quiet good-bye.

Now Mama was ready. She had held out until she was 91 years old, arthritic, and blind. She called my brother to come for her.

MITZI AND HER MEN
By Erika Hoffman

No act of kindness no matter how small is ever wasted – Aesop

It takes her a long time to get ready. Her hair must be shampooed. All tangles and knots removed. It requires frequent brushing. A bubble bath relaxes her before the date. She must look perfect, be perfect.

When she prances in, all eyes fix on her. Although she belongs to another, the men with a twinkle in their eye crave her attention. "You're a doll baby," they coo. Eager arms reach out toward her. She carries herself with grace and pride, seemingly aware of stealing hearts.

"Come over here, Honey. Sit a spell with me," a soldier urges. "I've missed you!"

"Let me take a good look at you." Another cups her face in his hands.

"That pink bow! Precious, you are!" Mitzi glows with the flattery. She parades and sashays around the room of admirers. Her primping has paid off; she's the center of attention, the belle of the ball. They ignore sports on TV to spend time with her.

"Sweet thing! Come over here! Come to Daddy!" They want to cuddle her, nuzzle her, stroke her hair. "You have beautiful eyes!" one whispers in her ear.

"Give me a little smooch, Mitzi." Sometimes she does. They laugh. They forget their pain.

"May I hold her?" one implores. "You want to stay with me?"

Mitzi snuggles with the old warrior. He laps up her gentle presence.

Every vet thinks he is her favorite.

Once a month the patients at the Durham VA Medical Center anticipate Mitzi's dolled-up arrival. They yearn to see her now as they gladdened in yesteryear to spot the USO supplied starlet.

Mitzi, the adorable girl in question, is a brown-haired beauty with big affectionate eyes, a loving nature, and a Farrah Fawcett mane! She's a shitzu who cheers up the veterans as her owner, Sheila Mann, a DAR with Caswell-Nash Chapter, looks on lovingly, knowingly, and proudly. She understands the allure of her charming creature and the ease with which these men fall in love with the petite, the sociable, the charming Mitzi, the Scarlett O'Hara of the Shitzu World.

My friend dutifully carried Mitzi to Durham once a month so her doggie could schmooze with the patients at the VA, be they nursing home permanent residents, or temporary ones. Sheila provided this service with her Shitzu because my friend is not only a kind person but also a grateful person, and she does not want any American serviceman no matter how stooped, blinded, or debilitated by age to think him or herself forgotten.

Mitzi was only a puppy when Sheila took on her care. Her mother-in-law, on her death bed, asked her to take the dog. At the time, Sheila was busy with a demanding job and precious little time for herself let alone a dog, but she granted her husband's mother her wish. Mitzi soon ingratiated herself.

Sheila's dad had been a vet. And after he passed, she wanted to do something for the men who ended up at the VA. She went through the rigmarole of getting Mitzi approved as a pet volunteer, which means certain documentation from the veterinarian as well as rigid vetting by the staff at the VA to determine that the dog is safe, affectionate, and well-behaved around older and sick people. Besides her monthly visits to cheer up the old soldiers with her pooch, Sheila also conducts Bingo Games. She recruits other DAR members to accompany her to serve soda, non-sugary snacks, and donate prize money.

Yesterday, I accompanied her to meet her obligation to have the Bingo game.

"I'm sure the VA coordinator would understand if you didn't feel up to going today," I told Sheila.

"We had to postpone it last week till now because of the snowstorm. The guys would be terribly disappointed if we don't have it."

So, we rode the 30 minutes to the VA Hospital which is very near Duke's Medical Center. We had to idle in a long line to gain admission to the parking deck. Sheila fretted about being late because she knows the staff has to wheel several members in and hates for the guys to be kept waiting in the rec room.

She and I grabbed the refreshments and scurried from the deck through the long skywalk into the building. She raced up the stairways since that was faster than cooling our heels for an elevator lift.

When we burst through the room, three other fellow DAR's were there.

"Let's do it!" Sheila announced and began introducing each of us as I started filling up plastic cups with ice and diet soft drinks.

"We're going to give each of you a dollar just for showing up!" Sheila announced to the crowd. Some of the old guys smiled. One stuck his in the bill of his hat. I distributed drinks with another "daughter" and then passed out individually wrapped crackers always giving them a choice as to whether they wanted ones that were cheesy with peanut butter or ones with cream cheese and chives. Some stashed the snacks away in their pockets for later. A wife sat next to one man who had tubes running from his nose and everywhere. A jovial granddaughter patted her granddad on the back as they both looked excited to be there ready to start the Bingo game. A staff member hovered over one more. Several vets put their cards right up to their noses since they were blind. We positioned ourselves throughout the room of twenty patients so that we could aid those needing help. A young staff member called out each number twice, using the microphone.

"Now this first game of Bingo is for five dollars!" announced Sheila.

How they concentrated! I stood between two who occasionally did not catch the numbers called or mistook "N60" for "N50." Easy to do!

One wouldn't think a faint voice could be tinged with glee! But it was! BINGO! One of us "daughters" scurried over and read off the winning numbers, and then the staffer verified with a "Good card!" And Sheila scooted over and handed a crisp $5.00 bill. With that winner finished, the others continued for several more "Bingo's" until all the $5's had been awarded.

"Clean your cards! Now some $2.00 games," declared Sheila. And, they played on with many more winning. The hour shot by. Such happiness. Fun.

"OK! Clean those cards for the last time! Now for the cover-all game!"

"All the boxes must be covered!" announced the staffer with the mike. The air crackled with a buzz of anticipation.

"This is for the $50.00 prize!"

"Wow!" I emitted. The guys smiled and looked intensely back at their cards.

I followed closely as I hoped my two had a chance. They were both down to only two spaces left vacant when an exuberant BINGO rang out from the one woman vet in the room! Since this lady is blind, Emily—a DAR - read out the letters and numbers.

"That's it!" said Sheila and she awarded the vet her prize. The winner clasped her hands together in utter joy!

"I think I was more excited even than she was!" said Emily.

Karen, Catherine, and I all agreed we had as much fun as the vets by just watching them play and compete for the grand prize.

One little old guy signaled to Sheila, and she walked over to him. "You're Mitzi's mom?"

Sheila's eyes glistened. She nodded yes.

"Did you bring Mitzi?" he eagerly asked.

Sheila shook her head no.

The men hobbled out of the room, or propelled themselves out, or were pushed back to their quarters.

We cleaned up. I told my pal how much I enjoyed it and I'd volunteer again.

"I really appreciate your coming with me today, Erika."

"No problem."

"And tell your husband how much help he was -- lending us that oxygen tank."

"Sure thing."

"It made her breathing much less labored."

Before we exited Sheila spoke a minute to the person in charge of volunteer activities who reminded the new volunteers that they didn't have to pay for parking. She turned to Sheila.

"Now when's Mitzi coming? The men were asking me."

I looked at my friend who glanced down. "I'll call you later today," Sheila replied, looking flustered.

As we descended the stairwell, I turned to Sheila, "You okay?"

"I'm actually better off than Allen. He's taking it hard."

"Seven years is a long time. You grow attached. You did everything you could. She died in the arms of the people who loved her. That is more than most folks can hope for," I said.

"We buried her yesterday on the farm Dad left me. And some day our son will inherit that land. We want to put up a stone bench and put some inscription on it about Mitzi."

"She was a real trouper."

"That she was!" said Sheila. "She was a good girl."

OUR CANINE FAMILY MEMBER
By Francine L. Baldwin-Billingslea

While out doing our Saturday shopping, my mother suddenly suggested that we stop by the pet adoption center and look at some dogs. We had been talking about getting one, but I felt that having a pet would be somewhat of a hindrance at that present time. As I turned into the parking lot, I sternly reminded Mom that we were only looking. Under no circumstances were we going to walk out with a dog. But Mom was on a mission, and the way she smiled and nodded her head in agreement, I knew that if she saw a dog that she wanted, she was going to get it.

As we walked up and down the aisles of caged barking dogs, I was secretly thankful that they all were the complete opposite of what we had in mind. As we were about to leave, a teary-eyed young woman came in holding the cutest little puppy in her arms, who suddenly leaped out of hers and landed safely into my mother's. As Mom tenderly cradled him like a baby, I saw the immediate bonding between them.

Before I could say anything, my Mom yelled out, "We'll take him!" My heart and mind quickly and silently agreed. It seemed as if the whole situation was predestined; we didn't choose Max, Max chose us. Mom's mission was accomplished, and my previous statement was forgotten, so we became the proud new owners of the handsome, over-friendly, six month old, Poodle/snaughzner mixed male. We were given his papers, a record of his shots, food, bowls, leashes and toys at a too good to be true price. It was a work of fate at its best.

We were quite happy with the newest addition to our family, and I think he felt the same way about us. When we brought Max home, a different type of energy and a profound sense of purpose entered in with him.

Mom and Max quickly became best friends. They went for their walks and she spoiled him by taking him for a ride every day. He rarely left her side. It was such a pleasure to see the joy and change he brought into her life; having him as a companion was very therapeutic for her. It seemed as if Max was the missing piece to a puzzle. Now there was an unexplainable feeling of wholeness. Mom once again had something to nurture.

A year later when Mom very suddenly passed away, Max grieved right along with the rest of us. For awhile he even lost his appetite, and I'd often find him sadly lying on or under her bed. He was always around Mom much more than me, but now, I began to feel an extra special closeness to Max that I never felt before. Soon he became my protector, my confident, my company and my best friend. With him around, the house didn't feel so empty, and I didn't feel as lonely. It felt good to walk in the house and be greeted with sloppy licks, perked up ears and a wagging tail. I also began to look forward to our daily walks, it relieved my stress, helped me stay in shape, and meet the neighbors. Max even got invited to a doggie-birthday party.

My fiancé, Wilson, began taking him for his rides, and soon they became almost inseparable. It was good to see Max getting back to his old self again.

Max really thinks he's human, I guess he has that right since I treat him as if he were a child and Wilson and his buddies treat him as if he's one of the guys. It's hilarious to see Wilson driving down the road with his trusty sidekick sitting on the front seat next to him – with their buddies riding in the back. Everyone has finally stopped complaining about this seating arrangement. Those who ride with the two of them knows this is how it is, and this is how it's going to be, including me.

Max has such a delightful personality and disposition; it's hard to feel despondent around him. He's definitely a mood picker-upper, and he's so smart, sensitive and loving that if he senses that you're not at your best, he'll leave you alone, but he doesn't leave your side.

Not too long ago when I was diagnosed with breast cancer and lost my hair to chemotherapy treatments, you could see Max's anxiety and sense his concern. He'd cuddle up to me much more and he'd lick my hairless head. Sometimes he'd carefully climb into my lap, yapping and looking me straight in my eyes, as if he was asking me if I was alright. I'd pet him and let him know that I was. I guess it was his way of telling me he was there for me.

Some might think we go a little overboard when it comes to him, but that's because they really don't know Max. To know him is to love him, but he doesn't have to really know you to love you back. There's a lesson in that type of essential quality for us humans. His unconditional loveable manner with everyone he meets never ceases to amaze me, and very often makes us overly protective towards him. Like a naïve child, he thinks everyone is his friend.

So why is Max so special to me? Because I believe he was a gift left to me from my Mom. Max's love helped me get through several tough times in my life. He was a companion, good company and a real comfort to me after she passed away. He was also very protective over me when I was sick.

Today as always, he makes us laugh and he fills my "empty nest" syndrome. He's very loyal and such a joy and a pleasure for mid-lifers such as us to have around. He makes a big difference in our quality of life. And last but not least, he's simply a part of the family who loves and needs us, just as much as we love and need him.

THE TOUCH
By Carol J. Rhodes

It was his blue eyes that held my attention the first time I saw him. Nothing else about him mattered at that moment. Not the chocolate brown ears, or the long white whiskers, or his sleek, taupe-colored fur coat. I only noticed these later on when he began to rub my leg.

We had instant rapport. This beautiful creature who quickly won my heart became my confidant, my pacifier, my comfort. He knew all my troubles, knew when I'd had a bad day, knew when I needed his touch. Sometimes he would tell me his troubles, too, and then meow as if to say that nothing was ever so bad that a little tuna wouldn't cure.

I shared his space for nearly eight years. Then one day, he was gone. Almost as silently as he had come. But on very quiet, cold nights, he still walks across my bed, kneads the covers gently, and purrs.

MY MUSE
By Carolyn T. Johnson

I love writing at the lake
where the tranquil water
and the quiet of the day
compel creative prose to
cascade onto the page

Yet occasionally the prolonged
solitude stifles me
makes me crave affection,
interaction, connection

This yearning leads me to
walk the deserted boat ramp
where I cup my hands and
make loud honking noises

Emerging from his perch
my fine feathered friend
answers my plaintive appeal
flies in low over the water
paddles to shore
waddles up close
His massive white wings
suddenly unfurl around me
caressing my isolation into remission
then disappear into his goose down

His bright orange beak nibbles
at the crust of sourdough I offer
while his navy blue eye
focuses on me,
his friend

A WINDOW TO WISDOM
By Lynn Pinkerton

I have new neighbors who are quietly reminding me of the important truths about life. Just eighteen inches outside my upstairs window, an expectant pair of mourning doves has set up a nursery on the outstretched arm of a tall, swaying palm tree. And now they devotedly tend and wait.

The twosome carefully staked out the claim on their new residence a few days ago and the flurry of moving in began in earnest. From my front row seat, I watched with fascination as the pair demonstrated a deep allegiance to collaboration and teamwork. The male flew in bits of twigs and grass to the female, who artfully wove them into the nesting cradle for their new family. The afternoon the dwelling seemed satisfactory, both snuggled into their new home and began a ritual of tender nuzzling and cooing, presumably speculating about who their offspring would look like and what career path they might follow. The next morning only one lone dove sat vigil, warming the small, white pregnant eggs.

Intrigued, some quick Internet research revealed that mourning doves are monogamous and parenting is equally shared from the moment they set up housekeeping until their offspring take flight into lives of their own. Rarely leaving the nest unattended, they take turns incubating the eggs, with Papa taking the day shift and Mama switching places with him for the evening. Once the babies are hatched, they are nourished by pigeon's milk, which both parents produce. Looking their best seems to be a priority and I often see them taking a break to preen and clean themselves and their nest. Of course, I cannot be certain, but there seem to be no squabbles about gender roles and whose turn it is to get dinner.

Mourning doves seem to be risk takers of a sort, often building their fragile nests in precarious places. My two new friends are no exception. The spot they have chosen to homestead sits over thirty feet above the ground, balanced near the tip of a wide, waving palm frond.

Apparently the risk is worth the anticipated gift. Buffeted by gentle breezes and stormy winds, the parent on duty takes it all in stride, riding both with equal tranquility and confidence. It intuitively knows its purpose and stays the course to fulfill it.

Throughout the day, I find myself peeking out to see how things are going. Regardless of whose shift it is, there is always someone sitting there. Always. I watch and wonder at the steady force propelling such loyalty and unswerving attention to the common goal. With patience and persistence, these delicately designed beings sit with gentle optimism, certain that their steadfastness will birth new life.

I spend the day scattering my energies answering emails, making phone calls, chasing deadlines, worrying about where the stock market will close and reading books on how to live fully present in the moment. All the while, I am constantly aware of the little bird who rests serenely just outside my window, doing his part and trusting the process.

REMEMBERING SASHA
By Nikki Rosen

Her name Sasha
Helper in Russian
Not just a dog
A friend – protector – comforter.
She knew
She understood
What no one else could.
She saw
She stayed
Never left my side
Never left me alone
Like so many others
Parents, siblings, grandparents who left or died
Sasha
I needed you
Somehow you knew
Your presence my lifeline.
Sasha
DOG spelled backwards GOD
You're no longer here
In your place He became my friend – protector – comforter
He knows
He understands
What no one else could.
He sees
He stays
Never leaves my side
His Presence – my lifeline.
Sasha

You opened the way
The door for me to stay
To not run too far
To not fall to death
Sasha
Replaced by One
Who opened the way
The door for me to stay
To not run too far
To not fall to death
Who gave me life.
Sasha
Helper in Russian
Friend to me.

Previous published in FellowScript Magazine
(Inscribe Christian Writer's Fellowship)

RUDY ON A SATURDAY MORNING
By Gayla Chaney

First, there is a gentle nudge, then a little playful poking, his nose behind my ear, his breath in my hair, his tongue on my neck. "Not now. Go away," I mumble. Under different circumstances, this might be considered foreplay. But this morning, it is only Rudy needing me to wake up and let him outside. He is gentle, but if I don't respond soon, he will start to bark.

I never set out to get a dog. He just sort of happened to me, like gray hair or a factory closing or junk mail. Rudy showed up on my porch six months ago, a black and white cur, hungry, cold and whining, whose lineage was impossible to discern. I told him, "Go away... shooo... go home, dog," with as much success as I am having this morning. I ignored him for two days. I put up signs: FOUND DOG. And finally, after a week, I gave him a bath, put an ad in the paper, and issued him what I assumed would be a temporary name: Rudy.

There was a time in my life when I would have called the pound when no one showed up to claim a stray. I would have said to myself and to anyone else that might have been around, "I don't have the time or space or desire for this." Ironically, when I had that kind of will and self-determination, no dogs bothered parking on my front porch. Timing is everything.

Rudy was sent by the dog angel at just the right moment, when all my defenses were down, when I didn't believe that I could alter the smallest detail of my life, when I used all the energy I could muster just to brush my hair and teeth before going to work. There was no strength left to resist a dog.

It is Saturday, and I had intended to sleep late, but Rudy is whimpering. I will put him in the backyard and I will get back in bed and place a pillow over my face so the room will look dark and I will go back to sleep, I promise myself, as I push open the screen door for my dog.

Rudy is delighted to be outside, squatting quickly before bounding off to bark at his neighbors through the chain-link fence that stakes out the property lines. There is a Boston Bull Terrier on the east side and a large part-Shepherd, part-hyena on the west side, as well as a couple of cats over the back fence, all of whom immediately know that Rudy is out.

I stumble back to my bedroom, hoping Rudy shuts up quickly. It's not that I need more sleep. I've had almost eight hours which is more than I ever get during the work week. But I want more sleep because it seems like a reward, one I think I deserve. I put the pillow in place over my eyes and attempt to drift back to wherever I was before Rudy slobbered dog kisses down my neck. This is my power: resisting the pull of the day to come alive and participate in grocery shopping, laundry, writing out checks to pay bills, and the endless list of time-robbing preoccupations labeled necessities of everyday life by the sadists who run our society. Sleep, I think to myself, is my own form of civil disobedience.

I doze off and on for another hour before acquiescing to the call of the day and the sounds of activity outside. I hear the pounding of a basketball against concrete before it slams against a backboard in the driveway next door and a lawn mower start up down the street. I head for the shower because water in my face is like an official notification that I am no longer dreaming.

I shower and while my coffee is brewing, I go out and get the paper. I give a little wave to the two neighbor boys playing basketball, and they holler, "Morning, Miss Westin." I smile, thinking what good kids they are, and then I realize I sound like my grandmother, crediting them with virtue simply because they greeted me. Ax-murderers could have manners, I remind myself. I know for a fact that habitual liars can have manners and good looks, too, and at certain times, showing up on my front porch like Rudy when I have little resistance, can worm their way back into my life by saying something as inane as, "I thought you might like some company tonight." It's presumptuous, it's arrogant, and it's unoriginal. How does he know that I'm not expecting someone else or on my way out to meet a friend or suffering from a bout with food poisoning? Probably because time and time again, I open the door and invite him in.

In the light of day, I much prefer Rudy's company. Dogs are noble, loyal, honest, and reciprocate love and affection with total devotion. I think it should be the highest compliment in the world to be called a dog. I think if anyone ever calls me a dog again, I'll turn and tell them, "Thank you."

Rudy is scratching at the door to come inside. He loves to watch me eat breakfast and for being so attentive, I give him the crust from my toast. His tail wags in gratitude. "You're welcome, Rudy," I say as I read the headlines.

I used to feel completely overwhelmed reading the morning paper when someone other than Rudy shared my breakfast table with me. Fate dictated and we all were victims of circumstance, like an abandoned wheelbarrow, exposed to the elements season after season, doomed to rust, unable to move or change a thing, destined to simply wait. And for what? Someone to come and pull it out of the rain, to rescue it from the effects of time and nature and exposure to things it couldn't escape.

It's hard for me to picture what I did without a dog. Rudy is good company as well as being a great distraction, always nudging me for a gentle pat or a scratch behind the ears. Feeling needed is a thread that pulls us along when we might otherwise choose to stop. Or stay in bed all day. Or make ridiculous phone calls to someone who is like tasty poison, flavorful dishonesty. I might as well pour syrup over broken glass and then shovel it into my mouth with a spoon. I don't ever want to be that hungry again.

Rudy wants to go out, but he wants me to go with him. He trots to the front door and then circles back to the kitchen, letting out a playful yelp to signify his intentions. I get the leash.

"Come on, Boy," I say. "Let's go." We head for the door. He gets so excited when we go out together. We walk around the block, smiling and nodding at neighbors who are washing their cars, working in their yards, performing their Saturday rituals.

Rudy is the best company I could ask for today with the sun glaring down so bright that everything seems to sparkle with clarity, so bright that I need sunglasses. I don't know what I'll do tonight if the doorbell rings after I'm already in bed, someone strategically arriving too late to go out, suggesting that I need his company because he was unsuccessful at finding anyone else that needed it. Saturday nights are difficult, attempting to have a little pride and resist him on principle, or if he doesn't show up, wondering where he is.

We stop and Rudy begins to pant with his tongue hanging out as he surveys his surroundings. He turns his head to look up at me, his brown eyes meeting my own, and what I see in them I interpret as unrelenting, unambiguous devotion.

"You're such a good boy," I murmur. I reach down and pat him gently. Rudy licks my hand and for the moment, for this one sunny, Saturday morning moment, I can't think of anything better than this.

SUNSHINE SAMMY
By Annmarie B. Tait

Our dog Sammy came into our lives not merely on a whim while passing a pet store, but rather after years of pitching the idea to my husband with little success. When at last Joe changed his mind, I wasted no time unraveling the mystery of why. Instead, I made tracks to find us a dog and fast!

Lucky for us, a woman I worked with knew of an eighteen-month-old Yorkshire terrier that needed a good home, and I jumped on the opportunity. "I'll take him!" I said, sight unseen.

The day Joe and I picked up Sammy we were met at the door by his owner and the ear-piercing yelp of the fur ball that peered at us through a baby gate that held him back within the confines of a powder room. "He's very energetic," the woman said with a slight giggle as she opened the gate and Sammy tore past my feet like greased lighting.

I glanced over at my husband's pained expression just as Sammy came barreling back through the room. This time he careened in circles around my feet while yapping with all the enthusiasm of a toddler hopped up on a birthday party sugar high.

I smiled weakly and said, "He's so cute! Does he ever slow down?"

"Sure," she replied. "When he's asleep he slows down to a full stop."

I gulped, then bent over and picked up my new eight-pound fur covered wiggle machine for the first time.

Sammy belonged to me now. I buried my face into his fluffy fur and breathed in his fresh from the grooming salon scent. We left with Sammy, his crate, his dog dish, and a whole lot of hope that we hadn't made a mistake.

The early days were harrowing to say the least. Sammy, true to his "energetic" reputation, managed to gnaw chew marks on the rungs of several kitchen chairs and shredded decorative throw pillows like they were going out of style. Still my husband showed great patience with teaching Sammy to obey commands and behave. And Sammy caught on – eventually.

Though trying at the start, once I took Sammy over to meet my dad, fear of having made a mistake dispelled the moment they laid eyes on each other. No matter how many times Sammy accidentally sprang a leak on the carpet, made sport of chewing up one of my slippers, or *worse* in the early days, the happiness he brought to everyone especially Dad made up for it all.

By the time Sammy joined our family, Dad was well into his seventies and triple bypass surgery topped the list of issues that little by little ate away at the excellent health he enjoyed for most of his life.

When Sammy and Dad took up keeping company, Dad was still pretty spry. He took him for walks and played fetch with him in the back yard endlessly without ever losing enthusiasm for Sammy's puppy dog antics. Dad relished our unexpected visits or better yet, when Joe and I went on vacation and left Sammy in his care.

Dad played with Sammy all day long and spoiled him to his heart's content. At night Sammy slept contentedly curled in a ball at the foot of the bed and Mom put up with the syncopated rhythm of their nightly snore-a-thons. She always said it was worth it just to see the spring in Dad's step whenever Sammy came for a visit.

As the calendar pages turned Dad's health declined but seeing Sammy still brought him great joy. Dad grew weaker on a daily basis and Sammy's visits seemed the only thing that roused his enthusiasm. Every time I pulled into my parent's driveway there sat Dad in his easy chair looking out the window waiting for a glimpse of Sammy. And when Sammy poked his little head high enough in the car window for Dad to see, Dad's face lit up like a neon sign.

Toward the very end Dad no longer had the strength to do much more than hold Sammy on his lap and stroke his fluffy coat. But Sammy adapted with love, always behaving and affectionately licking Dad to show his appreciation. I have no doubt that Sammy sensed Dad's need for his affection and lavished it on him for every moment they were together. The last time I saw my Dad in the hospital he barely had breath left to speak but as soon as I entered the room Dad turned his head toward me and with a frail smile whispered, "How's my little buddy?"

For months after he died Sammy curled up in Dad's favorite chair with a sad sigh every time I visited Mom. He grieved the loss of my father as much as we did. This was one very deep love story.

Once Mom moved into a retirement community Sammy attracted a whole new group of friends with his appealing nature. Just walking into the lobby with Sammy drew Mom's new neighbors out from behind their locked doors with high hopes for an opportunity to nestle him in their arms and pet his soft fluffy fur. And the years passed.

Mom is gone now, along with Joe's parents, my only uncle, and, very unexpectedly this past year, my dear nephew. All were official members of Sammy's fan club.

Sammy carries on, still bringing sunshine wherever he goes, well into his own golden years now. When freshly groomed, he looks just like the puppy we brought home who raced non-stop around my feet. But he is not.

Now when we go on vacation we reserve pet friendly accommodations only. Leaving Sammy in the care of a kennel, even one that boasts luxurious amenities just won't do. Sammy needs the special loving care it was always his pleasure to give to so many.

He still weighs eight pounds just as he did the day we brought him home, but frail rather than feisty better describes him these days. Though he still has a mighty yelp and a frantic wag in his little tail whenever a treat is at hand.

Sammy knows this house so well his deteriorating eyesight goes un-noticed. Still, the vet insists it has diminished. His steps are slower and no jaunt up or down the stairs is ever attempted without sincere deliberation on his part regarding the necessity of the trip.

Having Sammy with me all these years has kept a little piece of Dad's spirit alive in my heart and for that I owe Sammy a debt of gratitude.

This July Sammy will celebrate his fifteenth birthday, and I must reconcile myself to the fact that some day he will leave us to go keep company with Dad once again. I expect Dad will be waiting for him with open arms and one colossal soup bone that Sammy can gnaw on from here to eternity. Or at least until I get there to join in the fun!

LITTLE OWL OF WATCHFULNESS
By Penelope Moffet

My cat is my Buddha,
I shall not want
dog nor fish nor fowl.
She sits in sunlight rocking slightly
dreaming of world peace
for all but spiders, moths and flies.
Her eyes are wise, she sees
into the marrow of my heart.
Her fur is warm, she grants it
to my fingers, rasps her nubbly
tongue along the ridged licorice
of thumb and knuckle.
Yea though I do call her Smoke
her name is God.
Though I murmur "silly child"
she is intellect made flesh.
She hears my pleas,
bestows her purrs.
Sweet she is to smell
unless she's guzzled too much milk.
Her claws are sharp but do not pierce
except when wind dervishes the yard
and she recalls her lost stepbrother,
the one who deviled her for years.
Then does mildness turn to madness.
Then do I pray for peace
which always doth return
eventually. She hums me into sleep
and then awake, sitting by my head,
blessing my bedside glass of water

with her honest breath.
Yea though I walk through the vale
of bitter tears at 3 a.m.
I shall not fear
for Smoke is here,
delicately nibbling at her toes,
warning away the rats of the past,
restoring my soul.

THE EAGLE HAS LANDED
By Edward Louis

"The Eagle has landed," I said confidently into the lobby telephone of a quiet Rio de Janeiro hotel. As I hung up, the desk clerk looked at me oddly.

"Just calling my wife," I nodded and began dragging my suitcase towards the elevator.

It was my safe arrival call back home – the importance of which had been drilled into me by my father as I was growing up.

It seemed I couldn't leave our property without hearing him bellow, "Call me when you get there." His desire to protect us was ever-present. "Watch where you're going" or "be careful with that" tripped off his tongue as easily as "hello."

As I grew up, got married and started my own family, I began to understand his need to know that nothing had harmed us when we were away from him. Life was good, but my job required me to do a lot of international traveling. Long flights, busy meetings and hotel rooms in foreign countries meant little time for me to watch over my family – or for my family to watch over me.

Before the advent of cell phones and email, personal communication from these locales was often inconvenient and always expensive. Instead of having a long telephone conversation relaying the day's events, a brief "safe arrival" call would have to suffice. I would call my wife, Wendy, and recite the famous words said by Neil Armstrong in 1969 during the Apollo 11 moon landing: "The Eagle has landed." With that simple phrase, she would know that I had gotten to my destination as planned and everything was okay.

As our kids grew up and moved away, she, too, would have her share of exotic travels – like to California to see our daughter or to Florida to visit our sons. No matter where she went, I could be assured of a safe arrival call with our signature phrase.

Over the years, we discussed the last trip either one of us would ever have to take – that trip to the "Great Beyond." We always said that the one who got there first needed to send back a sign that they had crossed over successfully – in essence, giving a "safe arrival" call.

More than 30 years later – and eight months after being diagnosed with pancreatic cancer – my wife took that final trip. The thought of any kind of sign was the furthest thing from my mind. But on the morning of her funeral, my sister and I spotted an eagle flying over our house.

It might not have been such a big deal if eagles were commonly seen in my area, but they aren't. It was the first – and last – time I had ever seen one in several years of living there. My next door neighbor, who is an avid bird watcher, also saw the eagle that morning and confirmed it was a rare sighting.

The eagle circled our home and perched itself in a large tree on our property. It stared down at us for the longest time – almost as if it wanted to make sure we saw it. "It's Wendy," my sister announced as we stared back at the eagle.

Tears began to fill my eyes as we watched it finally fly away. "I think you're right. It's her sign to us: the Eagle has landed."

Previously published in Hope Whispers (Whispering Angel Books)

OH FUDGE! ANOTHER NUDGE!
By Terri Elders

*A dog is one of the remaining reasons why
some people can be persuaded to go for a walk.* ~ O.A. Battista

From the first, I thought of him privately as Natty the Nuisance. My husband had picked up the puppy as a freebie from the Flour Mill, a local feed and hardware store where people bring unwanted litters. He'd been advertised as a Great Pyrenees mix, but he looked more like Heinz 57 to me.

"Look, isn't he a lively one?"

Ken set the black ball of fur on the floor and our usually aloof adult female Akita bounded over to nuzzle him. She immediately flopped on the floor and rolled over on her back so that he could pounce on her belly and gnaw on her ankle.

"I just know this mutt will be a great companion for her," Ken said. "She's been lonely."

I just stared at the rollicking seven-week-old pup. That's just what I needed... another creature to pick up after, a shaggy one, too. What a nuisance!

Besides the dogs, three cats also shared our house. I liked animals in theory, but Ken had been ailing for years, so feeding, grooming, walking and cleaning up after all of them fell on me.

I muttered through the weeks of mopping up messes until Natty was housebroken. I grumbled until he finally learned to lap water out of a bowl without tipping it over. He sensed I was not his fondest fan, and spent most of his time curled up in Ken's lap. When he got too big for that, he settled for resting his nose on Ken's knee as my ailing husband idled away his days watching reruns of *Gunsmoke* and *Cheyenne*. Whenever I walked into the living room, Natty would cast me a mournful glance, and then bound over to Ken's recliner to snag some petting.

The only time Natty ever came near me was when I ran a comb through our Akita's coat or cuddled a cat. Then he'd scamper over and nose my hand away from the other pet. If I ignored him and continued to groom or caress, he'd whine and whimper, and then poke my hand again, harder. A total nuisance, I'd say to myself, the world's biggest pest.

"I've never seen an animal that craved so much attention," I'd complain.

"Oh, he's just a puppy," Ken would say. "He'll outgrow it."

But he never did. Then last spring my husband died. In the days that followed, Natty's neediness quadrupled. He'd avoided me before, but now he wouldn't let me out of his sight. He'd track me from room to room, and if I settled down to read or to work on the computer, he'd immediately sidle up and start nudging my arm.

I felt sorry for him. Ken had been his constant companion. I know dogs mourn loss just as we humans do. Nonetheless, I didn't appreciate the annoying interruptions. I wondered vaguely if I should find another home for him, one where he could get all the attention he hungered for... maybe a family with children to play with. I had my Akita as a guard dog, so I couldn't figure out what purpose Natty really served.

Nearing his sixth birthday, which should be middle age for a dog of his size, Natty suddenly seemed to be sliding into an early senescence. I noticed that he spent most of his time in the backyard just lazing on the grass, watching the birds and occasionally barking as a truck passed the house. Where he used to shoot back and forth from the patio to the apple tree, now, if he even bothered to get up, he'd plod slowly across the lawn.

Kind of like me, I thought. But I'm well into my seventies and this dog was far too young to have severe arthritis as I do.

When I took Natty in for his annual checkup and shots, the vet didn't pull punches.

"No arthritis. He's pretty healthy. But he's overweight, and should lose around twenty-five pounds. I know it's hard, but see if you can walk him more."

I sighed. I needed to lose twenty-five pounds, too. I'd packed on weight during my husband's decline. In grief, I'd comforted myself with creamy casseroles and carrot cake. And though I lived on a country loop frequented by walkers, joggers and bikers, I found endless excuses to avoid walking that mile-long course myself. It was too hot. It was too cold. I was too tired. I was too old.

Twice daily I'd been taking the leashed Akita for a brief stroll up and down in front of my property, with Natty trotting along beside us. But I hadn't walked the mutt around the loop since his puppyhood.

The next morning I dragged out Natty's old leash. While I snapped it onto his collar he thudded his tail against the front door. At least one of us was excited. I put on my jacket and mittens and the two of us set out.

To my surprise, Natty confidently lead the way, keeping a steady pace, not stopping to sniff at every twig the way his Akita sister does. He marched ahead, tugging me in his wake, not even pausing when neighbor dogs scrambled to the front of their owner's property to growl their territorial rights.

To my surprise, I enjoyed breathing in the scent of lilacs on the fresh spring air, feeling my heart beat a little faster from the mild exercise, even running my fingers through Natty's coarse fur when I reached down to pat him in approval when he heeled rather than strained to chase a passing car.

The next day we did it again. Then again. Soon we settled into a routine. If I grow too engrossed in catching up on my e-mail correspondence, around 10 a.m. Natty will be at my side, shoving his snout under my arm. Or if I become too distracted by household chores, he'll plant himself by the front door and rumble until I remember it's time for our walk.

Nowadays I see Natty as a blessing rather than a nuisance. Though the Akita remains my bodyguard, my elegant and diligent protector, scruffy Natty has become my personal untrained therapy dog. Together we're striding into shape.

He's nudged me into a new lease on life.

Previously published as "From Nuisance to Blessing" in Think Positive (Chicken Soup for the Soul Publishing, LLC)

FALCON'S EYE
By Madana Dookieram

I look into your eye
And I see fire my old friend
You flying so high above me
Protecting my every step
Razing all those who seek to do me harm

On my arm,
You were such a good bird
Talking to me
In your ancient tongue
Looking at me with those fiery eyes
I trusted you with my heart
To fly above me
Protecting my every step

I still remember the sounds you used to make
When I was in my bed and you on your stand
Pride and joy you were of my house
In your gaze
You kept us all safe

I remember how we used to talk
How I kissed your feathers
And you fell in love
Such a sweet one
I adored your every step
How you used to make me chatter
Such a mischievous bird
Up to no good

Such a sweet, a wise one
With predator eyes
Looking for the next prey to devour
In my eyes
I still see you looking back at me
My pride and my joy
My ancient protector

So high you flew
So high to watch
To watch all those beneath you

I remember the endless chatter you used to make in the morning
When you wanted attention
The look you used to give me when you got none
It makes me giggle
Attention was all you sought
Attention was all I got
Such a spoiled one
You were too spoiled
You had an army full of people
But yet you wanted more

My spoiled one
My protector
Who flew high up in the skies
Watching my back
As we head out into the sun
Knowing my every step
Protecting my every ground
I think and I miss you
My falcon's eye
Forever will your gaze protects me
Fly high, mighty one
Forever protecting everyone

PURRING, HOW, WHY, AND WHY NOT
By Maren O. Mitchell

Like the push and swoosh of surf,
kneading our knotted emotions,
filling our need to be needed,
to be given comfort,
the gift of the purr
wells from primal throats,
songs vibrating out concentrically
dislodging our foolish fears and stifling sorrows,
offering impartial healing.

Beginning with a feline need
the domesticated roar blossoms
as oscillations in the brain, sending
cords the message: *Twitch, rate of 25 to 150 per second.*
Just breathe, the purr will continue, in or out.

Evocative as a scent revisited, deliberate as eating,
cats glide against our legs, lie in our laps, quivering
with happiness, fur perfume rising,
pulsing health into us,
wrapping us around their tails.
A touch is all it takes.
Oh would that we could purr our "Om,"
important second only to breathing,
blanketing
our terrible world with sanity.

WHAT YOU MEAN TO ME
By MiMi Q. Atkins

Lying here by my side, you have been a devoted friend,
when my sorrows threaten to sweep me away,
 it was you who helped me mend.
You'd perk your ears up and look into my eyes at my tiniest cry,
and walk over to me and in my lap you'd nestle, curl, and lie.
I'd hear your heart beating and smell your canine scent,
You'd lick my hand and smell my hair, helping me to forget.

Always faithful, yes you are even though you are timid and mild,
Nature is your land of liberty, as you roam and jump like a child.
The wag of your tail, the sound of your bark,
the pitter patter of your feet,
are all the sounds of your music that makes my life complete.

You were there to listen and you never said a word,
Secrets, I shared with you, others haven't heard.
My heart was broken but the day I found you I began to heal,
you mean the world to me and you always will.

STREAK: THE PARROT WHO LOVES ME
By David O'Neal

Streak and I love each other. We truly do. She's an eight-year-old parrot, about sixteen inches from head to tail - a good part of her is tail - and she is beautiful: jungle green body, bright yellow ring around the back of her neck, bluish-black on top of her head, large white eye patches with the feather tracks all Macaws have, yellowish brown eyes with very dark brown irises, mostly black beak fading into white at the extremities, shades of blue, maroon and burnt-umber in streaks in her tail. She weighs about nine ounces.

Streak is a shoulder-bird. Some parrot breeders advise against letting birds stay on your shoulder: for safety purposes, and so the bird doesn't become domineering. However, both Streak and I are comfortable with her on my shoulder; I know she likes being there and it's not a problem for us. Although when Streak doesn't want to get off, such as when it's her bedtime, she creeps around behind my neck and hunkers down into the small of my back where I can't reach her; sometimes she will just grab onto my shirt with her beak and feet and refuse to move.

When I am working at my desk Streak is either on my shoulder, on top of her cage, in the corner sitting on the jungle-gym perch I've made for her up high, or sitting in the plant hanging below the perch. Sometimes I find her hanging upside down in these places. Streak stands on my shoulder when I shave and often gets flecks of shaving cream on her face. Then we shower. Sometimes I put her on my shoulder or arm and direct the shower-water onto her; more often she stands on the shower floor and spreads her wings and tips sideways so as to get wet all over and under. If I am not showering, I put her on the shower floor and she wanders around until sufficiently soaked. Streak is always exuberant and lets out little shrieks of joy as the water tumbles over her; then she comes out looking drenched and ridiculous. Then I put her into her cage to dry off. Streak will also bathe in the bathroom sink. I turn the water on for her, adjust it to lukewarm, and down into the sink she goes, having fun. When she is bathing she likes me to be in plain sight.

We take naps together too. I sleep on my side and Streak stands watch on the side of my head because it is the highest place on the bed. Sometimes she wants to play first, usually with my ear, grooming it or digging out wax or grooming my hair. She will often "beak" me: a sort of rapid fire motion of her head, like a woodpecker. This behavior is a show of affection prior to regurgitating (although she seldom actually regurgitates). I might make her a cave out of pillows or take her under the sheet and play tent, or turn her onto her back and rub her downy tummy, which is like frayed silk. After a while she gets up on my head and stands still. As I doze off, I can feel the warmth in her little feet.

We also prance around the house playing horse. She joggles up and down on my shoulder and we talk to each other with clicking and clucking noises, shrieks and little cries. She likes this very much. If I stoop to pick up something she ends up hanging upside down and the effect is comical. If I sing she will sing with me; she is off-key but definitely sings and in a completely different, softer voice than usual. I take Streak, on my shoulder of course, for long outside walks, or bicycling in a park or wooded area when she holds tight to my shirt, or kayaking too. She likes all these outside activities. We have meals together too. I set her food out at the same time as mine and she eats some of both. She likes cheese, milk, dry cereal, toast, fruit and vegetables. It's a hoot to see her suck up long pieces of spaghetti. When Streak is full, she gets on my shoulder or, better yet, on my lap or, still better, inside my t-shirt. She likes to be under a shirt or sweater very much and will stay there for long periods of time. Streak is semi-house-trained. She vacates on demand if I encourage her by saying "poop, poop." At such times I will put her on the edge of a sink or trash basket which she will excrete into. Interestingly, she never poops when under my t-shirt or sweater; nor does she ever poop in the bed.

Her moderate screech upon waking in the morning is the same tone with which she calls to me. It is a plaintive whine and means "Come get me, I want you." Her normal voice, when playing alone, is a sort of pleasant multi-toned mumble. Sometimes, when by herself, I catch her practicing her entire English language vocabulary: "Kiss kiss," "poop poop," "step up," "I love you," "night, night," and "hello" (which sounds like "arrow"). She also speaks her own name "Streak" or "Streaky." When she is under the sheet, Streak will often coo like a dove. And sometimes, in her most affectionate mood, she'll say "kiss, kiss;" she also says "kiss, kiss" when I play with her too roughly and she wants to stop. To me these responses are a clear indication that she has emotions and that she knows the meaning of the words and when to say them.

I am bi-polar and have had cycles of debilitating depression all my adult life. Streak came to me at a time of serious life changes: divorce after a long marriage, closing down of my business, moving from the East Coast to the West. Streak has been my constant and loyal companion during these stressful times. I am sure that caring for her, playing with her, having fun with her has been excellent therapy for me and has helped to combat the big time blues. I like to think I am good therapy for her too. I never imagined such a mutual bonding relationship with a bird could exist. The intensity of the connection we have with each other is mind-boggling and has grown with time. I am not completely convinced that all captive birds are better off in the wild, as some people say – because it's a jungle out there and, as Tennyson said, "Red in tooth and claw." After all, Streak is happy, healthy, guaranteed food and shelter, protected by me (her flock), and cherished. So who can say if Streak would be better off trying to survive in her natural environment?

I am late middle-aged so there's a good chance Streak will outlive me. That's okay because I know that someone else will love and care for her too although she would certainly miss me. If Streak goes first I will be able to comfort her in her last days. She will like that. If I go first, she will comfort me in my last days. I will like that. Streak and I love each other, we truly do.

SILVER SAINT
By Deadra Krieger

Egyptian Mau cats are often regal, beautiful, and finicky about whom they socialize with. Syca was no exception. She was a beautiful creature; silver coated with black spots and emerald eyes. I bought her as a kitten from a reputable breed, and though I never gained that special place in her heart, she did love me in her own way.

I rented a small cottage one year from a kindly, older couple. Though the cottage was within sight of their home, it sat on acres upon acres of farm surrounded by a lush national forest. It was breathtakingly beautiful, especially in the springtime. When we arrived Syca was a full grown cat, and though she had been spayed, she demanded to meander in and out of our home as she pleased. There were no dogs, whizzing cars, or any immediate threats I could see; so I caved and let her have her way. Though she would disappear for hours at a time, I would occasionally receive a mouse on my porch rug as a gift of thanks for her freedom.

My landlords were spry for their age. The wife would come and go, and was even involved in working with national parks. This job would often take her cross country for weeks at a time. The husband, a retired minister, busied himself with gardening, chickens, and helping his son fix up old vehicles in a garage next to their house.

The day he had a stroke came as quite a shock to us all. My heart ached for him when he was brought home in a wheelchair, his gaze lamenting and forlorn. The doctors, he explained to me, had told him the chances of him walking unassisted would be slim if ever. His voice was stoic, unwavering, but I could see in his eyes that it had crushed him.

A few weeks passed in which his wife did all she could to make him more comfortable, but she was eventually called away to work again. His son would spend breakfast and dinner with him, but usually was so caught up at work during the day and in his garage all night that his father was left alone for hours. I would look out my window and see my landlord sitting in his wheelchair, his eyes gazing longingly at his garden. His depression caused him to slump further and further, taking his health with it. I did what I could to help; weeding the garden and watering it, feeding the chickens and gathering eggs, talking with him and reading him books. I would have spent more hours in the day conversing with him, but my own job sometimes ran ten hour shifts.

As the months ran their course I began to see less and less of Syca. No more presents were left on my rug. When she did come home, it was only long enough to eat before she'd slink out the door again. Finally, she didn't come home for a week straight. A better job opportunity from several states away came up unexpectedly, and I wanted to take Syca with me. Unfortunately I didn't know where to find her.

I began to worry and, on my day off, went to my landlord's house to see if they'd seen my missing cat. Before I even got through the door, I heard her gentle trill of greeting. She was sitting in my landlord's lap, purring loudly as he smiled down at her.

"She sleeps with me at night," he confided in me. His eyes were lively now; closer to the man I knew when first I'd moved in. "She started bringing me gifts of mice, even a shrew from the garden this week."

I knew I couldn't separate them. She had chosen him as her person. Her eyes met mine and I could see the thoughts going through her head. *You are kind, and I love you. But I am needed here, and I love this man too.*

I moved a month later. My landlord happily waved goodbye from his wheelchair on the front porch as I pulled out of the driveway, the beautiful silver cat resting contently in his lap. I missed them, but I never regretted that decision.

Time passed and with it came a new job opportunity back in my home town. It had been two years since I'd left, but I never forgot my landlord or Syca. One summer evening I drove out to the farm on a whim, hoping someone would be home. As I pulled up, I was pleased to see the garden full of growing vegetables, looking healthy and weeded, and chickens scratching around the yard.

My landlord, to my surprise, greeted me before I even got to the front porch. A broad grin covered his face, and as he walked out on the porch, I noticed he had no walker. Trailing after him was a familiar little silver cat with black spots and emerald eyes.

"I'm so glad you came." He waved a hand at the cat. "She did it. I can walk now, you see. It's because of the kitty you gave me. Mouser would demand I get up to let her out, or get her food from the cabinet. I didn't have the heart to deny her. Each day it got easier to stand and before I knew it, I was walking."

I smiled at the name he'd given her, thinking it suited her despite her regal bloodlines. That was several years ago, but I will never forget it. I've had other cats since then, each of them close to my heart. I often think of Syca, though, and how she knew instinctively where she was needed. One little cat did what doctors couldn't; she inspired a man to truly live again.

UNLIKELY DUET
By Cona Gregory-Adams

His "Mom" had taken her grandson
bungee jumping, and left me dog sitting.
Eli, a tiny black "Pom,"
two pounds dog, five pounds hair,
stared at me. His sad eyes
begged, "My mommy's gone,
what're you gonna do about it?"
In spite of mediocre ability
–What do dogs know–
I began to sing,
You Are My Sunshine.
Eli pointed his nose heavenward,
pursed his mouth,
and sang with me, his tongue
curled into a rose-tinted
petal of love.

PURRS, PAWS AND CAT SCRATCH KISSES
By Sheree K. Nielsen

Random thoughts raced through my mind as I pulled into a parking space at the veterinary hospital.

As I entered the reception area, an attractive young blonde girl greeted me.

"Are you Mrs. Nielsen?"

"Yes."

"Come with me."

We walked past the front desk to the rear of the building where the cats were kenneled.

"Here he is."

The technician unlatched the eye level cage and the black and white kitten hopped down onto a stainless steel cart, the top covered by a white terry cloth towel.

A beautiful Tuxedo, he was missing his right rear leg. I gently stroked his soft fur, as he nudged his cheek onto my hands while purring. The technician explained that a Good Samaritan found him on the side of the road, leg mangled and broken. Dr. Miller advised, "Patience was Key." Due to the cat's leg amputation, his body needed time to adapt.

What was I thinking? With three animals at home, we had no business adopting another, much less one with a handicap. No cat would ever replace my first cat Rory, who passed away six months ago due to a heart condition and failing kidneys.

Suckers for a cute face, my hubby and I adopted the three-legged kitty. Unhappy with the name 'Snarky' (given him by the girls at the animal hospital), we agreed a new name was in order. Flipping through the pages of a book of animal names at the local pet store, one stood out. *Tripoli.* The name rang balance and harmony – two elements missing in his life. We hoped to prove ourselves good parents.

The initial shock of meeting three other animals, two of them canines, made Tripoli nervous. He hid for days. Slowly, he ventured from under our king size bed to check out his surroundings.

Despite Tripoli's handicap, he became adept at maneuvering throughout the house. So he could reach his food bowl, we strategically placed the barstools next to the kitchen countertop making it a shorter distance for him to jump up.

Balancing his back leg in the center of his body, he mimicked a tricycle as he moved about to check out his 'new digs.' Able to outrun our other cat Scooby, he was as fast as a cheetah.

Mornings after breakfast I retreated to the computer room to check emails. Tripoli followed close behind, hopping up on my computer desk while I typed. Whenever I moved the mouse, his eyes followed the pointer and his paw reached up to touch the screen. Intrigued by his curiosity, he reminded me of my first cat, Rory.

One evening I caught Tripoli watching television. I placed a kitchen chair in front of the TV so he could be closer. I observed as he 'tap, tap, tapped' his front paw on the screen in an attempt to swat all the insects in a popular movie. I laughed so hard tears streamed down my face.

Most nights Tripoli lay by my side in the same spot Rory laid the last night before he left this world. Trip would place his front paw gingerly in the palm of my hand as if to say, "Don't fret Mom. You've got me now." His purring helped me fall fast asleep.

Tripoli loved to be held and would raise his front paw to tap my leg, cueing me to scoop him up for affection. Sitting tall, head slightly turned, he would glance at me with lemon yellow eyes. Touching my cheek was one of his favorite displays of affection. "Mr. Trip, may I please have a kiss?" I smiled as he turned his head in my direction and brushed my cheek with his cat-scratch kisses.

Tubs and water fascinated Tripoli. Perched on the edge of the tub, he would dip his front paw in the water and splash, cooing to himself.

Just like Rory.

An 'awwwhh' feeling rushed through my body when Trip went through the motions of attempting to scratch behind his ear with the leg that was no longer there. His right leg moved in synchronization with the back of his right ear. I always assisted in his insatiable quest to scratch.

'Blue' times, like the day my mom passed, Tripoli was there to console me. Hopping up in the recliner, he placed his paw into my hand as if to say, "It's okay Mom, I'm here for you." I soon discovered Tripoli was the perfect listener.

When springtime came, he yearned to be outside in the flower garden. Although we had acres for him to roam, he always stayed close by, loving on the Missouri primrose and Columbine the way he would cat-scratch kiss my face. It took several tries to coax him in the house after a sunny day in the garden.

Recently, Tripoli has taken kindly to messing with my hair. In the quiet of the house on a rainy evening, I lay on the sofa watching TV. Tripoli hovers, snatching a lock of my hair with his front paw, biting the strands. Secretly analyzing by color, he is removing all the gray ones that have unexpectedly popped up in the last few weeks. One smart cat!

Over five years have passed since we adopted Tripoli. While he cannot replace the memory of Rory, he constantly brings me joy and laughter. With his boundless energy, Tripoli has shown me how to remain positive in the face of adversity proving that three legs are just as good as four.

THE CALF
By Christopher Woods

Dawn, horizon red in the East,
Clouds created a low ceiling
For the speckled crimson sky.
I walked my retriever
On his constitutional.

Across a neighbor's fence,
I watched the cows,
A procession of sorts,
Coming up from the grove.
One by one they marched.
Coming up the rear was a brown cow,
And, trying to keep pace with her,
A baby calf born in the night.

My wife and I had come to the country
For the weekend, to await pathology results.
She had breast cancer surgery a few days before.
Our lives were in a kind of upheaval,
Not knowing what might happen next.
For the first time, I had thought about fragility
In a new way, how things might end.
I had no idea what the news might be.

Then, seeing this calf, still wet
And struggling on its floundering legs
To keep up with its mother,
I was struck by the cycle of all of us.
For a brief moment, the calf looked at me.
I knew I was the first human

The calf had ever seen.
He studied me for a moment,
Showed a primal kind of recognition,
Then looked away, back to its mother.
And I looked away, into the distance,
Unsure where and how it might be.

Previously published in Survivor's Review at survivorsreview.org

THE SENTRY
By Judy Kirk

I live with a four legged feline
who announces bedtime with a yowl
every night at 10:10 p.m.
She sashays into the living room from
some secret nook she's been curled up in,
acting put upon to be kept up so late —
oh-she-who-sleeps-all-day.
I am only 10 minutes into the news.

No, I say in a loud voice, I am not ready.
The yowls continue in ten second intervals
as she prowls 'round my chair like a tiger
stalking its prey. No, I repeat,
shaking my head like a fool talking to a wall.
She strolls down the hall and nibbles
at her food, but she'll be back.

When the news is over, I head for my office.
I'll just be a minute, I say, already reading an email.
She's temporarily appeased, bed is just around
the corner, and she stretches out next to my chair.
I close my laptop and move to the bathroom.
She paces. Emits a short yip of a meow,
so soft, I can barely hear it.
She yips again. And again.

In bed, I pick up my book and she takes
her place at the edge of the bed, heaven forbid
she'd curl around my body like a normal cat.
I turn off the light, and hear the soft thud
of her body hit the floor.
She leaves me during the night,
returns at break
of day to paw my face,
nuzzle my hand, meowing
her good morning and get up message.
I stroke her back, mumble softly,
I am not ready, and we begin again.

THE COLOR OF LOVE
By Martha Lavoué

My Jade isn't green
but the color of golden sand
she lays her head upon my knees
and waits for my hand
to scratch between her eyes
as she listens to my sighs
her head weighs heavily on my thighs
I begin to cry and her bold brown eyes
watch me with compassion
she knows not the cause of my passion
but her devotion is one with my emotion
I rub between her ears
and my tears keep on falling
they wet her nose, she sneezes
and I laugh and say to both of us
"Jesus, that's enough pain for today –
Let's go out and play!"

UNDERCOVER CAT LOVER
By Dwan Reed

"Look at this, Thomas. Isn't it exotic?" I leaned closer to my husband so he could see the picture of a Bengal kitten romping through tall, green grass. I flipped to the next page while I still had his attention, and a photograph of dainty Siamese kittens perched on the back of an overstuffed, chair appeared. "Aren't these too cute?"

My husband gently pushed the magazine aside, turned toward me and shook his head. "No." He mouthed the words with barely a sound, which meant he meant business.

I threw the magazine down and met his determination with my own. "I want a cat!"

"No." He said. "I've told you for the millionth time, I don't like cats, dogs, rats... shall I go on?"

"Please Thomas. It won't be any bother. I'll take care of it."

"Dwan, no. I don't want one of those hairballs in my house."

After fifteen years of marriage, I decided *no* was no longer an option. "Listen, Thomas, this house is as much mine as it is yours. I want a cat, and I want it soon."

The room filled with an angry chill as my husband sat like a frozen ice carving—arms crossed, face contorted in a scowl. This was my cue to back down, but I was tired of waiting, and so were the children.

After about five minutes, I cleared my throat. "What's it going to be? Are you going to be fair?"

Thomas, resting his head in his palms, mumbled, "Alright, you win. But keep *that thing* out of our room and off my stuff."

Elated, I ran to the stairs and yelled, "Kids! We're getting a cat!"

Our daughter was the first one down the stairs, followed closely by our son. "Yeah! We're finally gonna get a kitty. When, Mom, when?" They nearly knocked me off my feet.

I pulled my brood close, catching my balance. "We'll go to the shelter this weekend to see what we can find. Okay?"

The following Saturday, the children and I piled into the SUV. By the time we reached the shelter, we could barely contain our excitement and raced through the front doors.

A couple of hours later, we walked out with a gorgeous brown tabby kitten with black stripes and white socks. We named her Pip. Only three months old, she was small enough to fit into my cupped hands.

When we arrived home, I put Pip down. She didn't waste any time, immediately dashing through each room of the house becoming familiar with her new surroundings. Thomas moaned, "I can't believe *that thing* is in my house. I don't know if I'm going to be able to stand it."

The months passed, and Thomas complained about Pip's shedding, the cost of her food, and her early morning meows. He criticized her failure to come when we called, her long naps, and lack of fiscal contribution to the family. He said, "You know, dogs are more obedient and much smarter animals. I don't think that thing understands anything you say. In fact, she doesn't even know her own name."

Despite my husband's insolence, Pip routinely laid near his feet while he watched television. Sometimes he would look down at her and say, "Thing, what are you doing there? Move. Go." But each time, she would look up at him with her big brown eyes and softly meow, as if to say, "Buddy, you don't bother me. I like you anyway."

By the time Pip was a year old, she had learned to come to the kitchen for her morning and afternoon snack. She even responded sometimes when we called. She played kickball with my son by moving a little ball back and forth with her paws. Thomas, surveying Pip's brilliant development into adulthood, began to call her *that cat* instead of *that thing*.

By year two, something curious happened. One day, I noticed Pip sitting next to Thomas while he worked on the computer in our home office. I watched the two sit peacefully, and noticed Pip's occasional gazes of adoration toward Thomas. From a distance my husband appeared content with her presence. At first, I thought this serene moment was only a coincidence, until I witnessed the same thing over and over again.

One day, I asked, "Thomas, I noticed that Pip has been sitting next to you in the office. What's that about?"

"Oh, I guess that cat just likes to be around quiet people. You and the kids are so noisy."

Three years have now passed since we brought Pip home and Thomas has shortened *that cat* to simply *cat*. He still complains when he finds hair on his suits and when she climbs on top of the kitchen table. He still claims to hate felines, yet when Pip arrives in the kitchen for her snack and no one is there to wait on her, it's Thomas who yells, "Feed the cat, someone. It's time for her snack. She's hungry."

When visitors come over, he's the one who says, "Our cat has quite a personality. She's sleeping right now, but she might come out before you leave." Or when Pip races through the house chasing imaginary critters, Thomas says, "Our cat is so funny. I wonder what she's thinking."

Pip taught us a valuable lesson. As our pets don't get to select their owners, we don't always get to choose who will be a part of our lives. Sometimes we're thrown together with those whom we feel no connection, and conflict ensues. Yet, we shouldn't lose heart.

Just like Pip, who sat quietly next to Thomas, enduring his barbs, when we practice patience and tolerance, even difficult relationships can blossom and flourish. Most of our associations have potential for growth whether they begin with a pleasant "meow" or a territorial hiss. When we make a commitment to show respect, impossible people become possible.

Pip's fortitude, kind spirit, and natural intelligence changed some of Thomas' preconceived notions about felines. Though it has taken three long years, Thomas and Pip have developed a special relationship. Sometimes I accuse Thomas of being an *undercover cat lover*, and he says, "Nonsense. That's just crazy. I don't like cats." Yet, his actions speak louder than words.

I hope that, like Pip, when I encounter obstacles in relationships I'll have the perseverance to paw through the barriers. And with Pip-like determination, we can all reap amazing rewards toward developing new relationships or rebuilding broken ones, despite our differences of opinion—or species.

RUNAWAY
By Mary Borsellino

A few days before my 26th birthday, my mother phoned me to tell me that one of my best friends from high school had committed suicide.

I'd moved away from the city where I'd grown up a few years before, and had lost touch with a lot of the people I'd known there. My mother expected that, because I hadn't talked to my friend in a long time, I wouldn't be too deeply affected by the news. But grief is a funny thing. It can hit us much, much harder than we expect. It can make us act in unexpected ways.

My grief made me run away. Not just a little way away, either. I lived in Australia. In my desperation to make sense of my friend's death, in a search for some kind of new meaning in the world to replace the understanding that I'd lost, I ended up in the United States. Sleeping on the couches of friends I knew online, I made my way from state to state.

California, Oregon, Utah, Colorado, Illinois, Michigan. As well as generous almost-strangers, who took in a soul-searching Australian and made her feel welcome, there was one other constant in every place I went: cats.

Every house I stayed in had cats. The students sharing a house on a hill in Salt Lake City had a cat, and so did the young couple and their new baby in the beautiful old apartment in San Francisco. The kitty in Portland was as round as a basketball, with black fur and white paws. In Chicago I watched a kitten chew on the wheatgrass growing in its little pot in the kitchen.

And as my journey went on, these cats began to teach me something about life. I saw them living in the moment, always ready with affection and attention when there were people nearby to give it, expecting only the simplest things to be contented: food, water, shelter, and love.

With my face buried in the soft grey stripes of a tabby, my sorrow felt different. It was still an ache of loss, but it didn't overwhelm my ability to see the good in the world. There were still things on earth that made sense. Love still made sense, and friendship, and cats.

After three weeks in America, I packed my bags a final time and boarded a plane back to Australia. I was ready to go home. I don't know if I would have been, without those cats there along the way.

NURTURING PAWS
By Paula Timpson

Nurturing Paws
paws are
nurturing
Touching upon Grace
paws strong, soft pads
walk Earth,
believing, giving pure Love
&
healing
to all
who dare
trust
in
nurturing paws-

THE LINK IN MY LIFE
By J.C. Howard

I'm not sure what final skirmish my father fought before he was pronounced dead, but he'd been carried from the field of combat long before the nurse called to tell me that his battles were over. Maybe the expression she used was expired, I'm not sure. He'd been in the nursing home for about six months, but he had left us before that, before he went to the nursing home I mean.

My father was over 6 feet tall and a muscular 220 pounds or so. He was a lean, robust man, in constant motion, with a handsome, wind tanned face. For him work and golf were both a religion. And in those two forums you could depend, that he never missed a day of work and played golf least twice a week. That I know of, he had a standing Wednesday game with his cronies and always looked to be a fourth on a Saturday pick-up game. He had never befriended weakness, in pleasure or work, and thought of it as a cowardly nemesis.

A straight-forward businessman is how I would describe my father. You knew exactly where you stood with him, whether in a business transaction or as one of his three children being counseled or disciplined at home. He seldom separated business from family. For my father, his family was much like a business; one he ruled and directed with similar guiding principles. Principles of honesty, charity, prudence, integrity, commitment, and love; all these and more guided my father, his work and his family.

That this rare form of "MS" came on slowly over a period of years was difficult for everyone to witness. It started when my dad lost his powerful stride and began walking strangely. Then as time passed, he slowly lost more and more of his motor control. Suddenly his condition deteriorated rapidly; the MS ravaged his body, and he no longer had the strength to transfer himself. He no longer could remain in a sitting-up position; his arms would gently flail about and it took great determination for him to simply keep his head from bobbling.

Uncomplicated tasks now became immense struggles against an invisible Goliath. He had become a prisoner within his own body and through the lens of a soldier's telescope he saw that he was losing the war. With all the strength in his soul, he had previously fought going into residential care, a nursing home, but now he required skilled nursing, it was no longer a choice of convenience. MS had become his mortal enemy and it feasted on both his physical and emotional strength, until he lost both those battles.

In this life of mine, there's some things I do know and there's some things I don't know.

What I do know is that my Dad died early on a Wednesday morning. I know that for a time, only my dog Lacey, could console me. I know that I visited my Dad at the nursing home every Monday night for dinner and every Wednesday for lunch. I know that I was his only daughter and the baby of his three children. I also know that he seldom recognized me during my visits in the nursing home.

What I don't know is how or why he forgot who I was. I don't know if it was a fever from an infection or out of control blood sugars. I don't know if it was a covert cancer in his brain, refusing to allow him to remember. And I don't know if his life had become so unbearable that he graciously declined to remember.

I do know that he remembered Lacey in those last few months.

I didn't know I only had those last few months.

I do know that we both loved Lacey.

Not unlike my own father, but as a parent to a four legged child, I also thought that my girl hung the moon. Lacey and I attended puppy classes, then intermediate classes and easily advanced to novice classes all before she was one year old. She grew from being the last of the litter, skinny, little, runt puppy into a beautiful 110-pound tri-colored, golden eyed German Shepherd. And had 110 pounds of a "knowing her own mind" temperament to go with it. At age one, she was among the best and the brightest. She was striking and effortlessly demanded attention whenever entering a room. I decided to share her enthusiasm for life with others less fortunate then ourselves and so... she became a certified therapy dog. Although she was as strong willed as she was muscularly powerful, her slow and easy kisses were the real giveaway to the size of her heart. And underneath her heavy, glossy, soft coat, she was all heart.

For years after she became certified both she and I would visit children's shelters, group homes, attend special fundraisers for different local handicapped communities and speak to misguided youth at our local juvenile detention center. She was loved everywhere we went, and I loved bringing her to as many events and scheduled visits as we could each month. Small children hugged her big thick neck and screamed in delight as they touched her cold, wet nose. Older children loved Lacey's powerful looks. They were thrilled to see her skill in obedience and were always caught off guard with her tender kisses. Lacey and I challenged ourselves to fight the battles for children with "pet therapy," as we brought cheer to young children and sensibility to teens, already deep in their own personal conflict.

I didn't know that Lacey and I would be fighting one of my father's battle with our therapy.

I didn't know that Lacey would be the link in my life that my father would remember and share, but she was.

I noticed early on after my dad came to the nursing home, that he began looking at me with a kind of a wild look. His uncombed hair and bushy eyebrows made him appear mad-man like. Maybe he was confused, I'm not sure. But he was no longer the calm, loving man that dried the tears of my youth or the dominant, authoritative man that guided my life into adulthood. He became jumpy and was easily agitated. My father, the man who was the epitome of self control had vanished. On one of my first visits, I remember clearly how he looked at me and then asked if I was a friend of his wife's. When I explained that I was his daughter, he asked again if I knew his wife, then turned away, turning up the volume on the TV. When this happened again the following week, I grieved the loss of my father.

Taught by my father to be charitable and not easily defeated, I decided that I would also visit other residents who possibly had no family. It only made sense that I would get permission to bring Lacey on my Monday night visits. And so it began, my relationship with my father in the nursing home.

On my first Monday night visit with Lacey, he looked squarely into Lacey's golden eyes, then at me. He studied my face for what seemed an eternity, then with a broad smile, he tipped his head and asked where we'd been for so long, saying how much he missed us both. Through Lacey, I had won an important battle that day for my dad and selfishly for myself. I don't know that he actually remembered me as his daughter, but I do know he recognized Lacey as my girl. Mondays became special for us. Each week my father and I would talk about golf, commitment, charity, love, and dogs; all the important things a daughter wants and needs to talk about with her old Dad.

THE CHOSEN ONE
By Nadia Ali

Walking around the Humane Society's enclosure there were all kinds of cats and kittens that were beckoning us with their pitiful meows. The watchful big eyes of cats followed our every move as we passed by. I hadn't told my daughters we were going to the Humane Society that day as they had categorically stated, "We don't want a replacement cat!" But that was six months ago when Tigger their childhood cat never returned home and left them with a void that I believed needed to be filled.

My mind drifted back to yesteryear and I could see my daughters as little girls running inside to tell me about the kittens their father had just found in our apartment building.

"Mommy, Mommy, come and see what Daddy has!" Their little faces full of excitement, grabbing on to my hand, pulling me to see.

There, in an old cardboard box, were three kittens huddled together barely opening their eyes. I remember the girls were scared to touch them, even though they wanted to stroke them.

The kittens were abandoned and the mother never came back. Only one kitten was chosen to stay with us as our pet. One went to a school friend and one to a neighbor. Tigger was the chosen name for our little kitten. He became my daughters' best friend. They shared their secrets with him, brushed his hair as much as they brushed their own and, of course, spoilt him.

The weeks turned into months, the months into years until two years later Tigger never came back home. My daughters used to come rushing through the door after school asking, "Mom, is he back?" My only reply was that Tigger was somewhere out there. Every day for a long time they asked. I could see their hopes were fading as time went by until one day, they asked no more.

As the weeks passed by, something faded from my daughters' eyes: a certain twinkling, a certain excitement that was alive when Tigger was around. Six months had passed and I took the first step to restoring their love and passion for having a cat as a pet as we walked around the enclosure looking at cats of all sizes, ages and colors.

"Girls, did you find anything?" I asked my daughters who had trailed behind stopping at each cage.

Raisah, the younger one, signaled to me to come over. As I approached, Shazara, the older one, turned around with tears falling down her cheek, "Mom, I can't do this. I don't want another cat!" She said softly wiping her tears away with her hands.

At that moment I knew that maybe I was pushing too much, so we turned, ready to leave. Just then one of the attendants came up to us, "Didn't find one?" she asked. "There's more over here," she continued, directing us over to a rather large enclosure at the back.

"We were just leaving," I responded, but the attendant still led the way.

"It's just here," she encouraged.

We reluctantly followed, having had our fill of the cats. The enclosure had lots of cats and a few kittens. As I walked across the front I remember thinking that they all looked so sad and desperate hoping someone would take them home.

I turned around to see where the girls were but they had stopped right at the very corner of the enclosure and were bending down stroking a kitten. As I made my way towards them, the attendant followed.

"Like that one?" she said happily, opening the cage and picking up the kitten and placing it in Shazara's hand. There was a sudden change of expression on her face. Her whole face lit up with sheer delight as she held the tiny kitten in her hands.

"Arhh look how cute!" she said. In my opinion, the tortoise colored kitten was a scrawny big-eyed kitten that looked undernourished. It squeaked at a very high tone and its claws were like needles.

"Really?" I questioned, as I watched the kitten claw its way onto Shazara's shoulders.

"She's a lovely kitten," said the attendant, "and you're lucky because someone nearly took her yesterday." The girls surprisingly looked at me as though we simply had to take the kitten home.

Before I knew it, I was signing the necessary documents to take the scrawny, big-eyed kitten home. Over the course of the day or so the girls named the kitten 'Cici.' She was quite an independent little kitten who had a personality all of her own. She disliked being held, when she wanted something she would meow at a high-pitched frequency and her eyes bugged out like they were two sizes too big for her head, but my daughters simply adored her.

For the most part Cici is spoilt, being allowed privileges that Tigger never enjoyed. She knows how to get things she wants with just a flick of her tail and a murmur of a meow. She has created a unique bond with all of us in some form or manner.

I can see the joy and inspiration that Cici has given to my daughters. That twinkle in their eyes and the excitement on their faces has grown from strength to strength. The hurt of missing Tigger become engulfed by the healing love for Cici, who has brought her own unique personality and behavioral traits. At the grand age of eight years old she is no longer that scrawny, big eyed kitten, but a beautiful, loved member of our family.

SPECIAL VISION – NOT SPECIAL EFFECTS
By Rebecca Groff

My neighbor's cats had three full-time jobs: eating, napping and hating each other, but when the time came, Puddy, Sambo and Hal knew what mattered.

Bonnie suffered from Crohn's Disease, an affliction that zapped her physical and mental energies. After their son left for college, she and her husband decided to get a cat to keep her company while he was away at work.

Into their life came Puddy, a solid white, long-haired female cat with celadon eyes and full Prima Dona attitude. Nothing was too good for "the Puds" as Bonnie called her: a fancy collar, painted ceramic feeding dishes, real fur mice toys, pricey tinned food, and plenty of catnip. Puds' eyes flashed psychedelic green after a "rolling taste" in the weed. Bonnie would spread a small pile of it on the carpet and Puds licked her paws before coating them with the kitty drug and 'getting crazy,' as they say. The weed transformed her into Wonder Cat as she pursued her dancing wire dangle toys and furry mice with evil passion. Those wild and crazy moments dulled the edge of daily solitude and delivered welcome fits of laughter for Bonnie.

Puds frequently stretched out close to Bonnie in the TV room, resting companionably in the warm panes of sunshine through the double deck doors. Even more often, though, the cat burrowed in alongside Bonnie on the sofa, the two of them napping long afternoon hours away in front of movies playing on the television. Soap operas, talk shows and news programs cannot compete with a warm, snuggling animal.

Bonnie's deck was outfitted with numerous bird feeders dangling from bordering bushes and small fruit trees, along with bowls of food conveniently placed out there for visiting strays. This is how Sambo entered the picture. He started showing up on her deck every morning for breakfast. Puds watched him through the deck doors, tail twitching, hissing when he stuck his nose up to the screen. Sambo watched back, unfazed by her attempts at intimidation.

One day Bonnie noticed a tear in his ear. Sliding the double doors open she coaxed him inside. The wound was treated, healing soon after, and Sammie -- as she called him -- and Bonnie sealed a friendship. Puds didn't approve of this, of course, but they learned to compromise. Puddy moved her cat-nap act into the formal front room of the house whenever Sambo was inside. Bonnie nicknamed it the "Throne Room." Complete with mahogany furniture and brocade sofa and chairs, it seemed the perfect place for the White Princess. *(No boys allowed!)* And Sambo never tried. Being with Bonnie was enough for him.

His beautiful moss-green eyes kept watch on the outside world while perched atop an oversized quilt next to Bonnie on the arm of the sofa. Come nightfall, however, he demanded — and received — egress out the patio doors for his favorite nighttime activities, but he always returned at daybreak to spend the day with her.

I don't remember exactly where Hal came from, or why Bonnie gave the young tiger-striped gray male that name. He just started showing up at the deck door each day, inspecting the feeding dish, and Bonnie couldn't resist, of course. One morning the deck doors were opened and in he came -- to stay.

Sambo had conspicuous eagle talons for claws, and there isn't a doubt in my mind that he could've whipped Puds or Hal with one paw tied behind his back, but he never did. I'd like to think they created a silent pact between them, possibly out of respect for the one who showered them with appropriate doses of love and vittles.

Hal seemed relegated to "adopted cousin" status. He'd curl and respond under the love of Bonnie's hand, but there was no pillow throne for him, and he didn't seem sure where he stood in the household. Resembling a young, fun-loving teenager, he often tried to entice Sambo off his perch. Sambo eyed him with a "don't you do it" green stare, but Hal kept pushing the envelope and finally the older, bigger cat sprung from his cushion, chasing the young punk out through the galley kitchen, around the sun porch, back through the kitchen, finally returning to Bonnie, who enjoyed bouts of hysterical laughter at such scenes.

Point made, Hal would take up his only real seat in the room -- Bonnie's husband's leather recliner. Sambo resumed his nap next to Bonnie, the brief entertainment over. But the circus could easily start up again if Hal decided to venture into the Throne Room, only to come flying back out with Prima Dona Puds close behind, hissing and spitting, poised to slap. Hal never really did get it: Throne Room: Puddy's. Daytime pillow next to Bonnie: Sambo's. Always.

Bonnie's body grew tired of its fight with the disease, and eventually a hospital bed was set up for her in the TV room. The cats took turns sniffing and inspecting this new dynamic in the room, but they never jumped up onto it with her. And then the day came when she no longer needed it.

Several weeks later after her death I stopped to visit her husband, and he shared a fascinating story with me.

As Bonnie's breathing grew shallow the morning she died, all three cats walked into the room, lined up on the floor by the head of her bed and sat quietly looking up at her, and waited. Bonnie's husband reminded me how those three had hated each other from the time they met and that he'd never seen them sit that close together before. After Bonnie released her last breath they got up and walked out of the room -- each going their separate direction.

The Creator gives animals special vision and talents to comfort, even teach, in mysterious ways that we humans lack for all of our ability to verbalize and rationalize what should be obvious. Puddy, Sambo and Hal put their differences on hold while they gave Bonnie one final gift: peaceful air in which to leave.

SERENITY
By Linda Blasko

I love the way
You cuddle up
And as you start to purr
I close my eyes
And sit real still
Trying not to stir
I try to find
That special place
You always seem to go
Content with life
And filled with joy
Somewhere I want to know
As time goes by
It seems quite clear
You are a part of me
We've traveled to
Another world
Where our souls are free

LITTLE TINKER
By Jean Varda

Short little legs running
up hills on the end of a leash
wearing a flashing red light
on your collar
so cars could see you
barking at everyone
that stopped in front of
the house
rubbing your nose in the cat box
knowing it was wrong
leaving little tootsie rolls
on the kitchen floor
"Bad Dog"
upstairs to pee in your bed
when I shouted at you
jumping four feet in the air
when it was time for a walk
sitting for hours in the window
waiting for me to come home.
And food, especially meat
and rich protein food
how you wolfed it down
not even chewed first
Now you are an old lady's dog
you sit contentedly on her lap
watching old movies for hours
you press your nose into
her old lady scent
she feeds you "goodies,"
little portions of her senior meals

she lets you out to pee on the
end of a long leash
you are her happiness
you healed her with your cuteness
you are the perfect dog

THE BEGINNING
By Kellye Blankenship

Each breath strengthened small new lives
Twelve; blinking once, twice, amazed my eyes
Dependent, helpless, searching secure
Scent urged by warmth sends the lure
Survival embraces instincts within
Self Preservation thrust to win
Scooping gently the smallest of these
Abandoning stress my aim to please
Caressing fur, holding close to my cheek
A lick of "thank you" arrives so meek
His breath of newness arrives just in time
My day disappears forcing pressures behind
Sharing moments while evening hours fade
Inhaling once, more fulfillment I'm paid
Returning the favor I lend him once more
To the new little family in hopes he will soar
The day complete I watch while they sleep
Twelve little puppies, all I will keep

NEVER TOO LATE
By Ronda Armstrong

My husband Bill and I chuckle as our two cats zoom past us and skid to a stop by their wicker toy basket in the corner of the living room. Tiffy's gleaming white fur swirled with brown and gray offers a striking contrast to young Teddy's gray coat with bold black stripes. Petite Tiffy and her giant pal bat toys out of the basket, pounce on them, then streak across the room again. Teddy takes the lead and Tiffy's on his tail, limber and quick for her advancing years.

We once doubted Tiffy's ability to adjust to another cat. When I mention this fact to Bill he says, "She's our mighty Tiff, a tough old gal!"

The seventh of our cats, Tiffy has reigned as the smallest and most sensitive. She moved in when she was five, along with her buddy Gilligan, because the animal clinic where they "worked" as greeters closed its doors. We promised to adopt Gilligan, a tuxedo cat, also age five. When Tiffy -- then named Iffy -- had nowhere to go, we took her in too.

We wasted no time changing her ambivalent-sounding name to one with more flair: Tiffany, shortened to Tiffy.

Occupied with our demanding lives and caring for three older cats, we failed to give Tiffy credit for her spunk, evident from her first night in our home. She hunkered down in a big wooden bowl on top of the refrigerator; she wouldn't be disturbed since our older cats no longer jumped that high. On the other hand, Gilligan spent that night and subsequent days under a bedroom dresser.

Tiffy reacted skittishly to our large cats who showed their advanced age with their awkward gaits, decreased energies, and shorter tolerance levels. They required attention, treatment, and medicines. She held her own -- although anxious, she showed pluck by familiarizing herself with her new surroundings. She remained cautious, yet somewhere near; her quiet and nurturing presence always available during the final days of our older cats.

Six years after Tiffy and Gilligan moved in, an unexpected change markedly transformed our view of her.

Gilligan died and left a huge hole in our three hearts. For the first time in twenty years only one cat greeted us when we arrived home -- Tiffy.

What now? Neither Bill nor I pictured her adjusting to a new cat.

Although Tiffy possessed a feisty side, she was easily upset. Gilligan, a sweet and gentle cat, had complemented her quiet dependability. Neither Tiffy nor Gilligan wanted to be the top cat after the last of our older cats died. Instead, they lived peacefully as co-cats.

Gilligan's death fell three weeks after we'd heard the numbing news about his fatal illness. His loss added to a series of family illnesses and treatments. In addition, my preparations for early retirement increased demands on my time.

In the midst of our unsettled lives our home grew too quiet. The truth lurked: we missed Gilligan.

We gazed at each other with questioning eyes before asking, "What should we do?"

"Other cats will show up; they always do!"

"Someone will call with a stray cat."

"Should we go to the animal shelter?" Bill asked.

"I don't know... do you think Tiffy would adjust?" My voice trailed off.

For a week Tiffy stayed close, ready with her quiet comfort. Soon her typical soft voice grew louder, more intense, and more frequent. She claimed our attention by persistently pawing at us, then she stared us down.

Her actions implored, "Do something!"

She settled our dilemma. We didn't need patience; we needed action. While we drove to the local animal shelter we pushed aside our fears and prepared to choose a compatible cat.

Teddy hooked us instantly with his contagious charm and roaring purr. He snuggled in Bill's lap, then later batted toys with unconfined enthusiasm.

Still we worried about Tiffy. Would she take to an energetic, hefty, two-year old cat?

When we returned home, she strolled to the living room to look at him in the carrier. For a moment, she growled softly. She circled the carrier and stopped in front to stare at him again. She glanced back at us with an expression that said, "Yes, he'll do." She sauntered from the room to finish her nap.

Over the next week, Tiffy watched Teddy race and play. He abided by her wish to have distance. To our surprise, within a few days she followed him wherever he went and did whatever he did. With his gentle manner he gave her loving pats, licked her face, and drew out her playful side. They entertained us with their friendly romps and tussles.

Without a doubt our petite princess proved us wrong. She did not have a tough time adjusting to a cat almost ten years younger and twice as big; she adored her giant pal. When she embraced Teddy so easily, we recognized our error in discounting earlier signs of her hardiness and nurturing abilities.

We realized in retrospect that Tiffy had seen us through not only the loss of four cats, but also other deaths -- my husband's parents, the remainder of my parents' siblings -- as well as significant changes associated with our early retirements and the medical issues we faced. She stuck to Bill's side, acting as a constant source of reassurance, when he was diagnosed with mantle cell lymphoma and subsequently had a stem-cell transplant. She did the same for me when I had flare-ups of Carney Triad, a rare tumor condition.

Over the years, Tiffy transformed from the soft-spoken, quietly present companion to one who positioned herself in the middle of everything. She made sure Bill and I paid attention, not only to her but also to possibilities for us to model her ways and change our patterns.

Our little Tiffy taught us a big lesson. New circumstances hand us chances to shine in ways we previously had not.

In retirement Bill and I turned hectic work lives that drained us into lives with a comfortable pace suitable for our levels of energy. We set aside time to keep dancing, our longtime outlet for exercise and fun. Beyond dancing we shared similar inclinations about how to spend our time: promoting kindness and helping others. Although we had survived health crises, we didn't want to engineer projects like raising research money or running support group meetings. These worthy causes were too taxing for us. We resolved to say "no" to most requests and "yes" to the ones we felt a strong stirring to do.

We honor our preferences for doing good one to one. As we learn about needs, I write cards and letters. Bill makes calls and runs errands. We visit. We deliver meals. We pray. Individually-focused efforts reflect our caring presence.

Tiffy approves. She sits quietly with us while we rest after finishing one of our caring contacts. With her example we strike a balance: care for others; care for ourselves. Old patterns give way to new ones.

Tiffy sits beside the computer as I write, daring me to persevere as I pursue my passion for writing. She punctuates her presence with loud meows to insure I notice her. Her head bobs to follow the words bouncing on the screen. She flips her tail, fascinated with animated figures and splashy color. After awhile she turns to butt me with her head, signaling me to break. She encourages me to balance energy needs and my writing dreams. As possibilities develop I consider them.

Without Tiffy I might have delayed offering my work to major sources. But I didn't. When *The Des Moines Register* and *Chicken Soup for the Soul* began publishing my essays and stories, I gained confidence in my ability to write positive messages. Initial successes motivated me to join a writing team responsible for writing meditations posted on a weekly blog, expanding my opportunities to inspire others.

As Bill and I age, Tiffy journeys with us; she's still dispensing her comfort as well as a resounding dose of her opinions. Along with her, we explore the delights and challenges of aging. Teddy plays his role too. As Tiffy's sidekick, he keeps her acting young. He uses his limitless curiosity to interest her in everyday wonders. What works for her works for us too.

When Tiffy joined our household we wondered how we'd manage with this small, reserved, sometimes anxious cat -- a seemingly unlikely candidate to aid our healing through the turmoil of change, loss, and illness. Today we wonder how we could have fared without her. The older she gets, the more she shows her hardy spirit: the small, but mighty Tiff.

We pat her and smile. "We're so lucky to have you sweetie."

She stares back with her determined look and emits a deafening, "Meow!"

We know exactly what she's telling us, "Never too late to pounce on life!"

RALPH
By Ben Humphrey

July 1, 1964 was my first day as a clinical associate assigned to 2 East, the children's cancer ward in the Clinical Center at the National Institutes of Health. This assignment was going to last one year. As a commissioned officer in the Public Health Service, I was serving my two years of military duty. All of the children on the ward had leukemia. Like the Vietnam War, leukemia in those days was a losing battle.

A nurse, April, introduced me to my patients. "Todd Yardley is a five-year-old. He's been receiving monthly chemotherapy for the last seven months. Nice kid. All you have to do is break the ice into his world," April said.

Todd was sitting in bed in the lotus position doing a puzzle, bald from chemotherapy. He looked me over, didn't smile or frown but stopped working on his puzzle. His bed was cluttered with plastic models of various breeds of dogs and lots of books.

"Give me five," I said, extending my open hand. He gave me a moderate slap, but the ice had not broken.

"This is your new doctor, Todd," Mrs. Yardley said in a reassuring tone.

Todd nodded; that was all.

I sized Todd up. I could get to this five-year-old, but I would have to figure out how to do that as the interview and exam went on.

Mrs. Yardley was articulate, which went with her modern librarian look. Her hair was pulled back, she wore horn-rimmed glasses and had a book in hand.

Todd was polite and cooperative but also cautious. After all, I would have to do a marrow aspirate on him this morning. Finally, I said I had just gotten a horse and asked if he had a pet.

"Yes," he said sitting up. "My friend named Ralph."

"Ralph?" I asked with a smile on my face.

Mrs. Yardley explained that Todd had had an imaginary friend name Ralph, and when the dog as a puppy came into their home, there had been a transmigration of a soul.

"Ralph can sit, shake hands and sort of roll over. I teached him that," Todd said, interrupting his mother.

After his mother corrected Todd's grammar, I asked Todd if he had some pictures of Ralph. Out from under the covers, Todd pulled an envelope full of photos of a Springer Spaniel. I sat on Todd's bed as we shared the pictorial history of friendship. There were pictures of Ralph as a puppy with Todd when he had a full head of hair, others taken later when Ralph looked full grown and Todd was bald. I was given a full description of each photo, and Mrs. Yardley didn't interrupt when Todd made an occasional grammatical error.

"Todd and Ralph were close enough before Todd was diagnosed, but now they are inseparable. We used to have a rule: Ralph was to sleep downstairs on his own bed," Mrs. Yardley said. Then she smiled, raised her eyebrows and continued, "Rules are made to be broken."

Todd filled me in on one detail after another, and I chuckled when I had to admit that Ralph was probably smarter than my horse.

When Mrs. Yardley suggested that Todd save some of his stories for tomorrow because I was probably busy, I told her, "No. Your son's stories are important. Good friends are hard to come by. They're the best kind of support."

"Yes," she said. "Todd was very withdrawn the first month after diagnosis. That's when Ralph took over. He was always present, always ready to listen to Todd, and some of the things I've heard Todd tell Ralph were..." she searched for the right words, "Well, they were very revealing." She paused again, "If those two want to sleep in the same bed, it's OK with me. I just wash the sheets more often."

For the next few months, I treated Todd, gave him his monthly chemotherapy and listened to tales of a five-year-old and his best friend. In August, I showed Todd a picture of my horse. In September, Todd proudly showed me a sequence of photos of Ralph rolling over. In October, Todd relapsed and lost his battle with leukemia in November.

One month after Todd died, Mrs. Yardley called. She was still trying to adjust but was doing better. When the conversation was almost over, I asked, "How's Ralph?"

"Well," she said, "Ralph moped around the house for over a month. I guess we moped around together, but he's recovered. He's now constantly at my side, and you won't believe this, Doctor Humphrey, but I talk to him, just like Todd used to. He's always there for me."

I told Mrs. Yardley that I believed her. I hung up the phone and thought there has been a transfer of support, and Ralph was back on the job, caring for someone else.

HOW MY CAT HELPED SAVE MY LIFE
By Aphrodite Matsakis

One morning a serial rapist slipped into my home.

It was a normal Sunday. Kitty sat by the sliding glass door to the backyard waiting for the doorman (me) to open it so she could go play on the patio. When I didn't come instantly she began meowing her "Hurry up! Can't you see I'm waiting for you?" meow. I tried to stall her because letting her out meant I'd be stuck "babysitting" her and I had groceries to put away.

Although the patio was enclosed by a six-foot fence, sometimes stray cats had jumped over it and tried to attack Kitty. Kitty, a declawed indoor cat with no fighting experience, needed a protector – me.

I wanted Kitty to be happy, but I had other things to do besides watch her sun herself and eat grass. As a compromise, I'd watch her for a while, go do a quick chore elsewhere, check on her, go do another little chore and so forth. I'd always leave the sliding door open a little so that she could run inside just in case an animal came onto the patio while my back was turned.

I never left Kitty alone for more than three or four minutes at a time. Little did I realize that it only takes that long for someone to quietly unlock the fence door, slip through the open sliding door and sneak into the house.

That particular Sunday I didn't feel like letting my cat rule my life. But Kitty was seventeen years old. She wouldn't be with me much longer, so I gave in to her. I was watching Kitty chase a bug when I remembered that I needed something from upstairs and galloped up the steps to get it. Within minutes, Kitty came galloping up the steps too.

I'd never seen Kitty run so fast in all her life, not even when she was a kitten. Now that she was older, diabetic, crippled by arthritis and weakened by heart, thyroid and kidney problems, her movements were usually quite slow and labored.

Then Kitty began circling around my feet making eerie sounds.

"What's going on?" I wondered.

Usually when Kitty was afraid, she'd go hide in the nearest closet. But now she had dashed up the steps like a wild woman and she'd never run in circles around me or made the kind of sounds she was making now. There were hisses and growls, but there was another element – howling; and her howls were combined with moans that seemed to emerge from the core of her eleven-pound body. Within seconds, their message, "Danger! There's evil in the house!" penetrated every pore of my body.

I flew down the stairs to check if indeed there was evil in the house and I saw a quite unfriendly looking man in my kitchen. I began screaming. I didn't decide to scream. The screams just came out, each one louder than the next, and the man fled.

The police arrived in minutes. My description of the intruder matched that of a serial rapist whom the police had been trying to catch for over two years.

"You're lucky," one of them said. "If your cat hadn't tipped you off, that man could have hidden somewhere and come up behind you. You'd have been caught off guard and he could have done whatever he wanted with you ... even killed you.

"But because the cat alerted you, you were aware and able to be on the offensive. The intruder didn't expect you to come down looking for him and – luckily – your screams scared him off. Whatever you paid to get that cat – it was worth it."

I hadn't paid a dime for Kitty. My daughter had seen her at an animal shelter and fallen in love with her. Over the years, however, I spent thousands of dollars on Kitty and was often called a fool for doing so. But now it's clear that I wasn't a fool at all. I helped to save Kitty's life and in return, that Sunday morning, she helped to save mine. After this incident, more lights were installed in the neighborhood and other safety measures were adopted. So perhaps Kitty helped others as well.

MY OLD LOVABLE NEW FRIEND
By Susan Berg

A funny thing happened to me just the other day.
The friendliest cat came to my door wanting to play.
He was meowing like crazy, peering in through the screen,
As if calling to someone it'd been a while since he'd seen.

I said, "Well, hello little kitty. What is it you want?
I've never seen you before. Are you just out for a jaunt?"
He was an orange and white Tabby with a depth in his eyes.
Of all the cats I've known, he was the most lovable guy.

As I petted him gently, he met my every touch.
He loved all the attention and just couldn't get enough.
I gave him some ham scraps and some water to drink.
He gobbled it all up; then was gone in a blink.

A few days went by when one night I couldn't sleep.
I stepped outside beneath the lamppost on our street.
I looked up at the stars as I so often do,
And talked to God and loved ones who are up there, too.

I thought I'd sure like to see that cute, friendly cat.
And right at that moment, he appeared! Just like that!
He came out from underneath the cars in our drive
And walked right to me. I couldn't believe my eyes!

We were both so overjoyed as if long lost friends
Who were finally able to embrace once again.
He squirmed with such delight at my every stroke.
In his eyes, I saw my friend Teddy – that's no joke.

You see, Teddy was my life-long friend who sadly died.
I miss him every day and often look for "a sign."
I asked the cat, "Are you Teddy?" Our eyes locked in a gaze.
Just then, as if answering, he raised one paw to my face.

He reached up with his paw and gently touched my chin.
It gave me goose bumps because I just knew it was him!
In awe, it took me a few minutes to take this all in.
Then, I said goodbye to my friend, "Hope to see you again."

The next morning in the yard he played wild and carefree.
He was running and jumping and climbing a tree.
That's the last time I saw him— don't know where he could be,
Or whom he belongs to, but I sure wish it was me!

I wonder, was it Teddy visiting me as a cat?
Maybe, just maybe? I'd like to think it was fact.
I'd sure love to see "my old lovable new friend,"
But, seems he's vanished—I haven't seen him since then.

If my friend ever does pay me a visit again,
I think I might keep him, if it is all right with him.

This poem is a true story about a wonderful, yet mysterious encounter I had with a most lovable cat that briefly visited me in 2003 right after my life-long friend, Teddy Lopez, sadly died at the young age of 42.

Previously published in Hope Whispers (Whispering Angel Books)

ABOUT THE CONTRIBUTORS

Sandra Ervin Adams considers poetry to be her saving grace. She has been published in anthologies and literary journals. She is listed in *A Directory of American Poets and Writers*. In 2008 she was mentored as an adult student poet in North Carolina's Gilbert Chappell Series and taught a poetry workshop at New Bern's First Literary Symposium. In 2006 she authored a chapbook, *Union Point Park Poems*. She has been a writer-in-residence at Weymouth Center for the Arts & Humanities, in Southern Pines, NC. Her second book will be titled, *Through a Weymouth Window*. Sandra lives near Jacksonville, NC.

Nadia Ali is a freelance writer born in London, UK and now lives in the Caribbean. Her work has been published both online and in print. Her writing credits include a feature in the 2011 Writers Markets Book. She is also a contributing author in the anthologies, *The Moment I Knew: Reflections from Women on Life's Defining Moments* and *Chicken Soup for the Grandmother's Soul*. She is an avid animal lover and has been published in *Cat Fancy, I Love Cats, Dog Monthly, Cage & Aviary Magazine, Bird Keeper Magazine,* and *the Florida Pet Book*. Contact her at nadiafreelancewriter@yahoo.com.

Diana M. Amadeo is a multi-award winning author who sports a bit of pride in having 500 publications with her byline in books, anthologies, magazine, newspapers and online. Yet, she humbly, persistently, tweaks and rewrites her thousand or so rejections with eternal hope that they may yet see the light of day. Visit Diana at her website at http://home.comcast.net/~da.author/site/.

Ronda Armstrong and her husband, Bill, live in Des Moines, Iowa. When not taking care of their cats, Tiffy and Teddy, they enjoy ballroom dancing and helping others. Ronda's stories appear in *The Des Moines Register*; in multiple collections of *Chicken Soup for the Soul*, including two new stories in *Inspirations for the Young at Heart*, forthcoming in August, 2011; and in anthologies about growing up in the Midwest from Shapato Publishing, *Amber Waves of Grain*, and Knee *High By the Fourth of July*. Ronda writes meditations, rotating with other writers, at www.thebridgemeditations.wordpress.com. Contact her at ronda.armstrong@gmail.com.

MiMi Q. Atkins was born Miesha Queione Atkins, in the quaint town of Albany, GA. She prefers the pseudonym, MiMi Q. Atkins in the literary world. She is a freelance writer, motivational speaker, high school English teacher and college instructor. She is currently working on her PhD in International Education. She has delivered powerful speeches and poetry readings at several schools, churches, and motivational events. She published her first poem at the age of 16 entitled Butterfly. She is currently seeking publication for her Christian-based series of children's books. She loves to read, write, and travel with her husband, daughter, and miniature Dachshund, Emerson. She can be reached at http://www.mimiatkins.com.

Francine L. Baldwin-Billingslea – I am a mother, grandmother, a breast cancer survivor and a newlywed for the second time around. I released my inspirational memoir, *Through It All*, in 2009. My recently found passion for writing has led me to be published in several anthologies, including *Chicken Soup For the Soul: Divorce and Recovery, Memories of Mother, Motherwise II, Liberated Muse, How I Freed My Soul Book I, The Rambler Magazine*, online for *Guideposts*, and a contributor to *Hope Whispers* and *Living Lessons*, also published by Whispering Angel Books. I love writing, traveling, and spending quality time with my loved ones.

Sara Barker spends her time helping young writers hammer out strong sentences at the charter school where she works in Wilmington, North Carolina. She has published essays in several anthologies and writes weekly articles for an on-line forum about parenting her two sons, Ellis and Thayer. She also works as a tutor, writing consultant, and freelance editor unless Daisy or Fontana has something more pressing, like a walk on the beach or a bellyrub.

Glenda Barrett, a native of Hiawassee is an artist, poet and writer and has been published in numerous publications. *Woman's World, Farm & Ranch Living, Country Woman, Rural Heritage, Whispering Angel Books, Mary Jane's Farm Magazine, Grand Magazine, Bread & Molasses magazine* and *Chicken Soup for the Soul* to name a few. Along with her writing she has been painting Appalachian scenes for forty years. They are for sale on Fine Art America at this time.

Susan Berg is a freelance marketing communications consultant with experience in the Chamber of Commerce industry where she produced award-winning newsletters and marketing materials. She has worked as an auto sports reporter, covering the racing events for the *USAC Western States Midgets & TQ Series* with articles published in *National Speed Sport News*, *Western Racing News* and *Racing Wheels*. Susan lives in Southern California with her family where she is working on her first children's book. For more information, Susan can be reached via email at ice.bergs@yahoo.com.

Justin Blackburn is an intuitive inner healer from Greenville, South Carolina. He has been published in various journals, reviews, zines, magazines. He has four books published. His last *Female Human Whispers of Strong Masculine Gentleness* was published in 2009 by Shadow Archer Press. He is also a performance poet who has been featured in venues from New Orleans to New York. Currently he is writing a book called *Enjoy The Irresistible Present*. His intent is to awaken everyone who reads it to a life of love and beauty! Justin Blackburn loves you. Find out more about Justin Blackburn at www.justinblackburnlovesyou.com.

Kellye Blankenship is a Christian, wife, mother, daughter, teacher, principal and author. Her life experiences were developed in the state of Oklahoma where social graces and good home cooking is a must. Her accomplishments are not her own. There were provided by the influential people in her life. If you are intrigued to know more, please inquire. She always welcomes a text at 580-303-8205, encourages an e-mail at kellyeblankenship@me.com and would love for you to visit her site at http://web.mac.com/kellyeblankenship.

Linda Blasko is a freelance writer and poet. Discovering the joy of writing at an early age, Linda's first written poem was selected to hang in the principal's office of her elementary school. This poem was written in memory of her precious 22 year-old cat, Brownie. Over the years she taught her how to be calm, allowing her to find peace and tranquility in those quiet moments spent with her. Linda writes personalized poems for friends and family. She especially enjoys spiritual writing and hopes to complete her first book in the near future.

Mary Borsellino writes because she feels miserable otherwise. Everything from music journalism to young adult thrillers has fallen out of her pen, and she doesn't plan on slowing down any time soon. She currently works as the editor for the Australia-wide not-for-profit journal *Australian Philanthropy*. Her website is maryborsellino.com.

Nancy Brewka-Clark's recent poetry has appeared in numerous collections including *Hope Whispers,* Whispering Angel Books, *Beloved on the Earth,* Holy Cow! Press, *Visiting Frost: Poems Inspired by the Life and Work of Robert Frost,* University of Iowa Press, *Regrets Only: Contemporary Poets on the Theme of Regret* by Little Pear Press and *Glass Works* published by Pudding House Press as well as *The North American Review, Orchard Press Mysteries, Tattoo Highway* and *Flashquake.*

Gayla Chaney's fiction has appeared in *Potomac Review, Concho River Review, Natural Bridge, Cicada, Thema, Carve,* and other literary journals. Her work has appeared in the following anthologies, *Best Modern Voices, Volume 2* published in 2008 by Wordclay Press, *Upstart Crows* published in 2010 by Wide Array Press, *Thank You, Death Robot* published in 2010 by Silverthought Press, and *Texas Told 'Em* published in 2011 by Ink Brush Press. She and her husband Phil enjoy the frequent company of their three granddogs, formerly wayward canines who all showed up uninvited but not unwelcomed.

Elynne Chaplik-Aleskow is an author, public speaker, and award-winning educator and broadcaster. She is Founding General Manager of WYCC-TV/PBS and Distinguished Professor Emeritus of Wright College in Chicago. Her adult storyteller program is renowned. Her nonfiction stories and essays have been published in numerous anthologies including *Thin Threads* (Kiwi Publishing), *Chicken Soup for the Soul* (Simon & Schuster Distributors), *This I Believe: On Love* (Wiley Publishing), *Forever Travels* (Mandinam Press), *Press Pause Moments* (Kiwi Publishing), *My Dad Is My Hero* (Adams Media) and various magazines, including the international Jerusalem Post Magazine. Elynne's husband Richard is her muse. Visit her online at her website: http://LookAroundMe.blogspot.com.

John R. Chega has been homeless most of his adult life. He is 58 years old and has been handicapped since 1978. The past two years have seen John publish over 25 articles in the *Calgary Herald,* the *Calgary Sun,* the *Drop In Centre* quarterly newsletter and *Street Talk,* a newspaper concerned with the plight of the homeless. Offering himself as a "Speaker" at conventions and topical gatherings John is committed to bringing awareness and understanding of what it is like to be homeless and how to help. His connection to the story "Pepper" is empathetic and heartfelt. Contact him at johnrchega@hotmail.com

Paul Cummins is the Executive Director of New Visions Foundation, the primary founder of New Roads School, a co-founder of Camino Nuevo

Charter Academy, Los Angeles Academy of Arts and Enterprise Charter School, and New Village Charter School. Prior to New Visions, Cummins was also the primary founder and headmaster of Crossroads School and founder of P.S. Arts. He is the author of several books, most recently, *Two Americas, Two Educations: Funding Quality Schools for All Students* (Red Hen Press) and *Why Poetry?* (Xlibris). Paul and his wife, Mary Ann are the parents of four daughters, two grandsons and one granddaughter.

Holly Day is a freelance writer and mother of two living in Minneapolis, Minnesota. Her poetry has recently appeared in The Midwest Quarterly, Pennsylvania English, and Coal City Review. Her recent books include *Music Theory for Dummies, Music Composition for Dummies,* and *Guitar-All-In-One for Dummies,* co-authored with Jim Peterik, former guitarist of the band Survivor. Her poetry has recently appeared in *Louisiana Literature, The Midwest Quarterly,* and *Coal City Review.*

Madana Dookieram is a Trinidadian born poetess and writer who currently reside in the beautiful Caribbean islands of Trinidad and Tobago. At present she is working on her first novel entitled *Lotus Flower* and you can reach her at her blog www.knowyourheart.wordpress.com.

Terri Elders, LCSW, lives in the country near Colville, WA with two dogs and three cats. Her stories have appeared in dozens of anthologies, including multiple editions of the *Chicken Soup for the Soul, A Cup of Comfort* and the *Patchwork Path* series. She serves as a public member of the Washington State Medical Quality Assurance Commission. In 2006 she received the UCLA Alumni Association Community Service Award for her work with Peace Corps. She blogs at http://atouchoftarragon.blogspot.com/.

Cristina Ferrari-Logan – After a rewarding and colorful career as wife, mother, chef, pianist, and teacher, I've arrived pleasantly intact at the Geezerette stage of my life where retirement affords me quality time to write. It's immensely satisfying to record and share memorable moents, some of which have been published, and all of which have made the trip infinitely worthwhile! My workroom décor is "Early Reject." Sometimes, when I'm writing, I pretend not to notice my little "assistant" raiding Grammy's Jelly Bean Jar while his older brother scans the mail for that eagerly anticipated "acceptance" letter. Hope springs eternal.

Kathleen Gerard is a prize-winning writer whose work has been widely published in magazines, literary journals, anthologies and broadcast on *National Public Radio* (NPR). Kathleen writes across genres and is the author of *In Transit* (a novel) and *Still Life* (a spiritual memoir). Several of Kathleen's plays have also been staged and performed regionally and off-Broadway. To learn more visit: www.kathleengerard.blogspot.com.

Sarah Goodwin-Nguyen is the author of *Key West: A Guide to Florida's Southernmost City* (Parkscape Press.) Her ebook on rabbit care, *The Pet Rabbit: From Head to Feet and Everything In Between*, is available for the Kindle or on Lulu.com. When not writing, she can be found rehabilitating wildlife at the Key West Wildlife Center. Visit her website: www.sarahgoodwin-nguyen.jigsy.com.

Cona F. ("Faye") Gregory-Adams is an award winning writer of poetry, children's stories, non-fiction, and short fiction. She has published in newspapers, magazines, poetry journals, and anthologies. She is co-editor of the *Missouri State Poetry Society Annual Anthology of Poetry and Prose*, published by the De Soto chapter, *On the Edge*. Faye serves as Contest Coordinator for the St, Louis Writers' Guild, and chairs the annual *Big Write* contest for 4th-8th graders. She lives in De Soto, Missouri with her husband, Billy, and two spoiled cats. View her books at www.fayeadams.com.

Rebecca Groff is a freelance writer for the Cedar Rapids Gazette. Her work has appeared in *Women's Edition*, *CountryEXTRA*, *Julien's Journal*, *Good Old Days*, and *Capper's*. She is a contributor to numerous anthologies that include *Cup of Comfort* as well as Shapato Publishing's anthology collection: *Stories About Growing Up In and Around Small Towns in the Midwest* (www.shapatoPublishing.com). She enjoys leading a monthly writing group for the Carl and Mary Koehler History Center in Cedar Rapids, Iowa, and she writes a blog at http://rebeccasnotepad.wordpress.com. She can be found on Facebook at www.facebook.com/Rebecca.Groff.

Erika Hoffman is the author of 88 published articles and non-fiction narratives which have appeared in nationally known anthologies and magazines.

J.C. Howard is a native Oklahoman with a Master's Degree in Social Work from the University of Oklahoma and works in the field of Children and Family Services. She is the founder of FurEver Readers, a local reading program for inner city children and a contributing writer for the children's advocacy site, www.theworldto1.org. She is a member of Oklahoma's Red Dirt Writers Society and Shotgun Story Writers. JC's long time best friend is her husband and her inspirations for writing are found amongst the events, people and beloved animals that share her life.

Ben Humphrey is a retired professor of pediatric oncology living in the Rocky Mountains. In 2005, he started writing and publishing poems. Several poems have been published in various American and European literary journals and anthologies, including *Trivial Pursuits* which appeared in Whispering Angel Books' anthology, *Living Lessons*. He is currently editing a memoir of his professional experiences caring for children with leukemia, which will include an expanded version of *Ralph*.

Carolyn T. Johnson, a former banker and now freelance writer from Houston, Texas, draws on her colorful life experiences in the US, Europe and South Africa for her short stories, poetry and essays. She writes from the heart, the hurt, the heavenly and sometimes the hilarious. She has been published in the *Houston Chronicle*, *Austin American-Statesman*, *Living Lessons, Hope Whispers, The Yale Journal of Humanities in Medicine, The Shine Journal, Della Donna, The Caper Journal* and *Tower Notes*.

Lynn C. Johnston is the author of *Angel's Dance: A Collection of Uplifting and Inspirational Poetry* and founder of Whispering Angel Books. Her poems and essays have been published in several anthologies, including *Forever Friends, Timeless Mysteries, Antiquities, The World Awaits,* and *Turning Corners, Bridges*. She served as editor for *Hope Whispers* and *Living Lessons*. Originally from New York, Lynn is a graduate of SUNY New Paltz. For more information, please visit www.whisperingangelbooks.com.

Judy Kirk, retired from a career in advertising, now writes poetry and teaches memoir writing classes at libraries throughout Minnesota. She has published two chapbooks: *Eclipsing the Gray* and *Straight Through the Heart*. Both focus on thoughts about growing older. Her poetry has appeared in several Whispering Angel anthologies and two of her poems were just accepted in Talking Stick, a Minnesota Literary magazine. She is a graduate of Indiana University and lives in St. Louis Park, MN.

Rosalie Ferrer Kramer is a published author, poet, and freelance writer. Her book, *Dancing in The Dark: Things My Mother Never Told Me* received many glowing reviews. Her work has appeared in *the San Diego Union Tribune* as well as many local papers. She has written regular column for the *Rancho Bernardo Sun* and made several television appearances regarding her book. Rosalie was the mother of two sons who died from Muscular Dystrophy and is now working on a book titled, *Saying and*

Doing it Right: With the Disabled, the Bereaved and the Fatally Ill. For more information, go to www.authorsden.com/rosaliefkramer.

Michele Krause is the Scribe of Four Harbors Audubon Society and regularly has her poetry displayed on their website (http://fourharborsaudubon.org/submissions.html) along with the poetry of her rescued hound dog, Quilliam Horace Flint, who recently published his doggerel -- the proceeds of which will benefit his shelter as well as three rescues of which he is especially fond. Michele is Horace's typist and also spends her time assisting several animal rescue organizations, especially Wetzel County Animal Shelter in WV and Make Peace With Animals Greyhound Rescue in the PA/NJ/NY area. She teaches high school English and has always loved to write.

Deadra Krieger has avidly been involved in animal rescue for more years than she can keep track of. She is a firm believer in the healing power of an animal's love and can be found living on the East Coast with her passel of kids, husband, two dogs and, of course, her cat. She loves hearing from her readers and can be contacted through her site at: http://dfkrieger@blogspot.com .

Martha Lavoué, originally from California, has lived in France for 40 years where she worked as a computer project manager. She writes poetry in both French and English and has been published in several literary journals and anthologies. She is inspired by simple everyday emotions and events, such as her dog grabbing her skin (gently) in her teeth to beg for breakfast scraps. She has also written a full-length book about her father's experience with McCarthyism, but no one wants to publish it. She can sing on key and paints decent watercolors of animals and people.

Edward Louis is a widower, retired executive and active member of his church. He is a father of three and grandfather of four. In his spare time, he enjoys exploring the world by cruise ship, spending time with his family and solving Sudoku puzzles.

Suzanne Manning – Since I was a young child, I had always dreamed of living in the country, having a baby, and owning my own horse. I am presently living my dream with my husband Joe, our beautiful daughter Serena Grace on a small farm in Massachusetts. I have always loved to express myself through my writings. I enjoy writing about my family and our animals. I have one Children's Book published called, *Tales from a New England Farmhouse, Matilda & Jeremiah*. I donated all the proceeds to two charities in honor of my 15-yr old-niece Jordana who is presently battling leukemia.

Aphrodite Matsakis, Ph.D., counseling psychologist, is an internationally recognized specialist in post-traumatic reactions. She writes because she "has to" and loves to dance. She's the author of *Back From the Front: Combat Trauma, Love and The Family* as well as 13 books on a variety of psychological topics and *Growing Up Greek in St. Louis*. She's also written numerous articles on psychological themes and on the Greek-American experience and has appeared on radio and television regarding combat trauma, sexual assault and relationships. For further information and for articles, visit her web page www.matsakis.com.

Mark McGuire-Schwartz sometimes imagines that he was raised by bears, and it shows. Mark has published poetry and prose in many journals, including *Caduceus, Fairfield Review, RogueScholars, Bent Pin Quarterly, Connecticut River Review, 6 Sentences, Whatever Literary Magazine, VerseWisconsin, Nanoism, Connecticut Law Journal*, and *On The Bottom of Rocks*. His chapbook, *Loss and Laughs, Love and Fauna*, was published by Oy Vey Press in 2009. Mark is the Co-Director of Poetry Institute – New Haven. Mark is currently developing a new poetic form, called the Seventeen.

Rosemary McKinley began writing to both entertain and inspire others. Her book, *101 Glimpses of the North Fork and Islands* was released in 2009 and led to interviews by radio station KJOY and the Suffolk Times highlighting her humorous classroom story and her book. Her short stories, essays and poems have been published online by the Visiting Nurse Association of Long Island and in *Lucidity, LI Sounds, Clarity, canvasli.com, Peconic Bay Shopper, Fate Magazine, Examination Anthology* and *The Ultimate Teacher*. One essay landed her a profile in the November 2006 issues of Money and Fortune Magazines.

Beckie A. Miller began writing after the death of her son at age 18 who was robbed and shot to death in 1991 to vent the horrific emotional aftermath of what murder left behind. She has been Chapter Leader of Parents Of Murdered Children (POMC) In Phoenix for the past 18 years, where she has served on many crime victims' organizations and won numerous awards for her service to crime victims. Beckie is a mother of three, grandmother of two, and wife to her husband, Don, of nearly 39 years.

Maren O. Mitchell – After living in France, Germany, and throughout the southeastern U.S., Maren O. Mitchell now lives in northeastern

Georgia with her husband and two cats. She has taught origami in four states, taught poetry at Blue Ridge Community College, Flat Rock, NC, and catalogued at the Carl Sandburg Home National Historic Site. Her poems have appeared in the *Red Clay Reader*, *The Arts Journal*, *Appalachian Journal*, *The Journal of Kentucky Studies*, *Wild Goose Poetry Review*, http://wildgoosepoetryreview.wordpress.com/, *Southern Humanities Review*, and elsewhere. Poems are forthcoming in *Pirene's Fountain*, www.pirenesfountain.com, and *The Classical Outlook*.

Barbara Moe is a freelance writer, who lives in Denver, Colorado with her husband and an occasional borrowed dog. She is a nurse, an adoption social worker and mother of seven, whose published work has included 17 non-fiction books for people (The Rosen Publishing Group) on various aspects on health/wellness, a textbook on adoption (ABC-CLIO), and a chapter book, *Dog Days for Dudley*, published by Bradbury Press.

Penelope Moffet's poems have appeared in *The Broome Review*, *Earth's Daughters*, *The Missouri Review*, *Steam Ticket*, *Wavelength* and other magazines, as well as in the anthology *What Wildness is This: Women Write about the Southwest* (University of Texas Press, 2007). A chapbook of her poetry, *Keeping Still*, was published by Dorland Mountain Arts Colony in 1995. She has work upcoming in *Permafrost*, *Pearl* and *Riverwind*. Smoke, the protagonist of "Little Owl of Watchfulness," lived to the ripe old age of 19. Moffet currently lives in Culver City, CA, with Emily, an peach tabby, and Raku, a snowshoe Siamese.

Elaine Morgan is an award-winning poet and freelance writer in Virginia. Her works have appeared in *HaikuPix Journal*, *The Poet's Domain*, *Wising Up Press*, *Earth's Daughters*, among others. She is a three-time Senior Poet Laureate for Va. through the Kitchener Foundation. Now retired, she shares her work in animal rescue and as a licensed wildlife rehabilitator through her writing. She recorded a CD *Raining Cats and Dogs*, a journey of memoir and poetry for those who love and lose their beloved pets, and she is currently working on an inspirational manuscript *Free To Fly*, about the spirit of the handicapped wild birds she kept as educational animals. raining530@yahoo.com.

Sheree K. Nielsen won the People's Choice Award, 1st Place for Non-fiction, Storyteller Magazine Apr/May/June 2010. A Missouri Writer's Guild member, she also serves as Publicity Chair and Photographer for Saturday Writers. Publications: *CHAMP Assistance Dogs*, *Cuivre River Anthology IV and V*, *Folly Current Newspaper*, *St. Charles and Monroe County Suburban Journals*, *Saturday Writers Newsletter*, *Caribbean Travel and*

Life (Postcards). Sheree freelances for *Missouri Life Magazine*; and is busy editing her inspirational essay collection. An active church member, avid scuba diver and sailor, Sheree resides in Missouri with her husband and three animal children. Learn more about her at www.shereenielsen.wordpress.com and www.oceanspiritphoto.com.

Linda O'Connell is a multi-published freelance writer, seasoned teacher and Member of Distinction with St. Louis Writer's Guild. Her humorous and inspirational essays and poems appear in numerous publications including twelve *Chicken Soup for the Soul* books, *Hope Whispers, Silver Boomers, Reminisce Magazine, Sasee Magazine* and more. She likes to think that she owns a dog, but in reality the dog owns her. Contact Linda at billin7@yahoo.com. Linda blogs at http://lindaoconnell.blogspot.com.

David O'Neal, a graduate of Princeton University who lives in San Francisco, is a retired rare book dealer now enjoying a second career as a writer. He has authored several books and written pieces on books, book collecting and biographies. His creative work has been published in several literary magazines and anthologies. He recently compiled and edited *Babbling Birds: An Anthology of Poems about Parrots, From Antiquity to the Present*, which contains 101 poems by Ovid, Statius, Han-shan, Tu Fu, Wordsworth, Rilke, T.S. Eliot and many others. O'Neal's website is davidloneal.us.

Lea Gambina Pecora – I've enjoyed writing since childhood. It calms me, and leaves me feeling simply blissful. My poem "Inspiration" was published in the 4th series of *Chicken Soup for the Soul*. Later, a producer wanted to use the story of my poem in a television episode. Since then, I've devoted most of my time to my family and business, and less on writing. Recently, life presented some undesirable twists, and writing has helped me through, and is here to stay. My hope is that what I create in words will impact others and enrich people's lives in a meaningful way.

Scott Peterson is the co-author of the book *Theme Explorations: A Voyage of Discovery*. His poems and essays have appeared in *The Plain Song Review, Home and Other Places, Beyond Forgetting: Poetry about Alzheimer's disease, Catapult, The Quarterly*, and other journals. He is a teacher-consultant for the National Writing Project and teaches writing classes at Western Michigan University. He lives in Mattawan, MI.

Lynn Pinkerton is a freelance writer who knew in the fifth grade that she wanted to be a writer when she grew up. Sidetracked by careers in social services and special events marketing, Lynn eventually reclaimed her childhood aspiration, joined a writing group and began publishing. In addition to other publications, her work has recently appeared in *The Christian Science Monitor*, *The Path* and *The Porch Swing* anthologies, *New Southerner* and *The Shine Journal*. She lives in Houston, Texas.

Paul Piper, a librarian at Western Washington University in Bellingham, received his MFA in Creative Writing in Montana. He has published four books of poetry including *Winter Apples* by Bird Dog Press. His work has appeared in various literary journals and books including *The Bellingham Review*, *Manoa*, *Sulfur*, *CutBank*, *The New Montana Story*, *Tribute to Orpheus*, and *America Zen*. He has also co-edited the books *Father Nature* and *X-Stories: The Personal Side of Fragile X Syndrome*. Visit his blog at: pipergates.blogspot.com.

Alan Pratt writes and tells stories for adults and children. He has published humorous essays and nature pieces, as well as poetry, for adults. He is the author of numerous children's stories and puppet plays. His picture book for young children was published in 2005.

Dwan Reed is a multipublished freelance writer with works appearing in *Chicken Soup for the Soul*, *Guideposts Incredible Prayer* series, and *Total Body* magazine. Dwan, who has her Masters in Social Work from Denver University and Bachelors in Psychology from the University of Missouri, is a women's prison evangelist and a professional public speaker. Visit her blog at dwanreed.com.

Carol J. Rhodes has won several literary aways for both poetry and prose. Her play, "Comin' Home to Burnstown," was showcased in a summer play festival of an off-Broadway theatre several years ago. She has written numerous short stories, essays, poetry, non-fiction, and plays, which have appeared in *Houston Chronicle*, *Christian Science Monitor*, *Stroud (England) News & Journal*, *The Houston Press; Country Home*, *Good Old Boat*, and *Texas;* as well as numerous journals and anthologies. In addition to creative writing, she occasionally presents business writing seminars for two universities and several corporate clients.

Nina Romano earned an M.A. from Adelphi University and an M.F.A. from FIU. She has taught English and Literature at St. Thomas University; writing workshops at Ft. Lauderdale Main Library, Sanibel Island Writers Conference and Florida Gulf Coast University. Her writing appears in many reviews, including: *Rome Daily American, Chrysalis Reader, WhiskeyIsland, GulfStream, Grain, Dimsum, Southern Women's*. Romano is the author of two poetry collections: *Cooking Lessons*, submitted for a Pulitzer Prize, and *Coffeehouse Meditations,* from Kitsune Books. Her short stories collection *The Other Side of the Gates* will be published by Kitsune Books. Romano has been nominated twice for the Pushcart Prize, and the SIBA Award. She co-authored *Writing in a Changing World.* Learn more at: ninaromano.com, bridlepathpress.com, and kitsunebooks.com.

Nikki Rosen began writing in 2008. Her first book, *In the Eye of Deception: A True Story* won The Word Guild National Book Award and received an Honourable mention for The Grace Irwin Award in June of 2010. She has written a few articles and stories that have been published. Recently her story, *A Refugee's Hope* won first place in a short story contest. Nikki lives in Canada with her family. She can be reached at blueheron12345@yahoo.ca or www.gentlerecovery.webs.com.

Ruth Sabath Rosenthal is a New York poet. Her poems have been published in numerous literary journals and poetry anthologies in the U.S.and abroad. In 2006, her poem "on yet another birthday" was nominated for a Pushcart prize. Ruth's debut chapbook *Facing Home*, published by Finishing Line Press, can be purchased from Amazon.com; full-length book of poetry titled *Facing Home and Beyond*, published by Paragon Poetry Press, Inc., can also be purchased from amazon.com and from paragonpoetry@aol.com. Learn more about Ruth's work: http://www.pw.org/content/ruth_sabath_rosenthal www.ruthsabathrosenthal.moonfruit.comand, www.poetryvlog.com/ruth sabathrosenthal.

Deborah Schildkraut, Ph.D. is an animal behaviorist, writer and advocate for senior dogs. Her column, *Casa Canine*, appears in *PETroglyphs Animal Resource Magazine*, www.petroglyphsnm.org/. Writing under the pen name of Bam Schildkraut, her children's books include *Goodbye, Jake*, and *¿Cuantos Perros? How Many Dogs?* which will be released Fall 2011. Find out more at www.bamschildkraut.com. Deborah's story, *Do Not Delete*, is dedicated to all of the older dogs who languish in animal shelters simply because of their age. She hopes you have the good fortune to bring a senior dog into your heart and home.

Paul Sohar started publishing in earnest when he went on disability from his day job at a drug company, namely in *Agni, Chiron, Kenyon Review, Phoebe Journal, Rattle, Rhino*, etc, and seven books of translations, but now a volume of his own poetry, *Homing Poems*, is available from Iniquity Press. *True Tales of a Fictitious Spy* is his creative nonfiction book (Synergebooks, 2006).

Tammy P. Stafford is a speaker and author of her memoir, *Labeled by Humanity, Loved by God*, a collection of personal miracles. She publishes a weekly inspirational newsletter. She's married to Steve and they have two daughters, Sydnee and Sloane. Her parents are Clyde and Juanita Parker. Check out her book page on facebook.com, website at www.tammypstafford.com or email her at tammy.stafford@hotmail.com

Willard Stringham is a writer from eastern Kansas. He has a degree in history from Avila University in Kansas City, MO. His writing has appeared in *The Upper Room, Snowy Egret,* and *The Mid-America Poetry Review* among others. He enjoys writing about animals and the environment. When not writing, Willard enjoys reading and watching golf.

Annmarie B. Tait resides in Conshohocken, PA with her husband Joe Beck and Sammy the "Wonder Yorkie". In addition to writing stories about her large Irish Catholic family and the memories they made, Annmarie also has a passion for cooking, sewing, and crocheting along with singing and recording Irish and American Folk Songs. Annmarie has in excess of thirty stories published in various anthologies including, *Chicken Soup for the Soul, Patchwork Path,* the HCI *Ultimate* series and *Reminisce Magazine*. You may contact Annmarie at: irishbloom@aol.com.

Rebecca Taksel lives in Pittsburgh, Pennsylvania, where she teaches French and English courses at Point Park University. She is a regular contributor to the *Redwood Coast Review* on subjects ranging from personal memoir to music, literature, and interior design. She was active for many years in advocacy for animals, writing for *Animals' Agenda* magazine and contributing a profile of a beloved Pittsburgh humane officer to *Speaking Out for Animals*, an anthology about people who rescue animals. Visit Rebecca on Facebook.

Paula Timpson – I am a published poetess. My son, Jamesey, is my muse! My website is http://paulaspoetryworld.blogspot.com. My poetry books may be found at Amazon.com. I write for God, everyday to bring peace and love to the world.

Tina Traster is an award-winning journalist/columnist/essay writer whose work has appeared in newspapers, magazines, literary journals, on NPR, *The New York Times, The New York Post, The Bergen Record, The Huffington Post, House Magazine, Hudson Valley Magazine, Mamazina, The Nervous Breakdown, the Mom Egg, Whistling Fire, The Feline Muse, Adoptive Families Magazine,* and more. *Love Learned,* an essay about bonding with her adopted Russian daughter, is anthologized in two collections:

Whispering Angel Books and Mammas and Pappas from City Works Press. Since 2006, Traster has written the *Burb Appeal* column for *The New York Post*. The columns have been anthologized in Burb Appeal, a paperback and e-book.

Jean Varda's poetry has appeared in *The California Quarterly, The Berkeley Poetry Review, Illya's Honey, Daybreak, The Lucid Stone, Poetry Motel, The Santa Fe Sun, Rive Gauche and Manzanita*. She has published five chapbooks of poetry, most recently, *Carved from Light and Shadow*, by Sacred Feather Press. Jean has emceed three open mikes and taught poetry writing workshops. She works as a hospice nurse in the Sierra Foothills and has hosted a radio show on KVMR, Nevada City, CA.

Louise Webster graduated with a B.A. in Communications Arts. Upon graduation, she worked at a cable T.V. station writing the evening news. Staying home, after the birth of her first child, she continued contributing work to many small presses and won a poetry contest celebrating the history of Lake Ronkonkoma. Louise also wrote for some of the more commercial magazines and anthologies. She wrote an article for *Garden Design*, a psychology text book, *Graces* and *Dog Blessings* by June Cotner, and is a frequent contributor to a science fiction quarterly.

Chuck Willman lives in Las Vegas. He writes poetry, enjoys painting, and hanging out with his best pal, Buddy (a 15 lb. Chihuahua that he rescued from a shelter). Chuck has several poems forthcoming in July 2011, in *Assaracus* (a new poetry journal from Sibling Rivalry Press), and is thrilled to be included in *Nurturing Paws*. He is an avid supporter of animal rights.

Wendy Wolf -- I live near Seattle with my darling, pinball-obsessed husband, and our adorably funny cats, who I love so much that I became vegetarian, then vegan, because I could no longer bear the thought of *any* animal being hurt or killed to feed or clothe me. Most of my poems are about animals and nature—moments I experience that fill me with wonder, or break my heart and make it bigger. Whenever I see the sort of kindness and devotion in the world that inspired "Black Dog," it lifts me up. And for that, I am deeply grateful.

Christopher Woods is a writer, teacher and photographer who lives in Houston and in Chappell Hill, Texas. He has published a novel, *The Dream Patch*, a prose collection, *Under a Riverbed Sky*, and a book of stage monologues for actors, *Heart Speak*. He teaches creative writing classes at The Women's Institute in Houston. He and his wife Linda are both cancer survivors. They share a gallery at Moonbird Hill Arts, www.moonbirdhill.exposuremanager.com.

Cherise Wyneken is a freelance writer. Selections of her prose and poetry have appeared in over two hundred journals, periodicals, and anthologies, as well as two collections of poetry, two chapbooks, a memoir, a novel, and a children's book. She enjoys reading her work at various local venues in the San Francisco East Bay where she lives. She is currently writing a weekly column on poetry for the Oakland online version of the Examiner: www.examiner.com/poetry-in-oakland/cherise-wyneken. Learn more about Cherise at www.authorsden.com/cherisewyneken or http://givingbooks2kids.com

WE WANT TO HEAR FROM YOU

Has one or more of the stories touched your heart? Has it made you think differently about your own situation? We would like to hear your thoughts or comments.

Do you have a short story or poem that you'd like to see in a future Whispering Angel Book? If so, please go to our website for upcoming book topics and submission guidelines.

Whispering Angel Books is dedicated to publishing uplifting and inspirational stories and poetry for its readers while donating a portion of its book sales to charities promoting physical, emotiona,l and spiritual healing. We also offer fundraising programs to help you increase revenue for your charitable organization. If you'd like more information, please contact us.

To contact us or to order additional books, please visit:

www.whisperingangelbooks.com

www.ingramcontent.com/pod-product-compliance
Lightning Source LLC
Chambersburg PA
CBHW031247290426
44109CB00012B/469